BANGKOK

TRAVEL GUIDE
2025

Explore Thailand's Capital, from Must-See Sights to Street Markets, Temples, Culture, and Practical Tips for Visitors

Donald M. Clark

All rights reserved. No part of this publication may be reproduced, distributed, or transmitted in any form or by any means, including photocopying, recording, or other electronic or mechanical methods, without the prior written permission of the publisher, except in the case of brief quotations embodied in critical reviews and certain other noncommercial uses permitted by copyright law.

Copyright ©Donald M. Clark, 2025.

Table Of Content

MAP OF BANGKOK... 7
Chapter 1: Welcome to Bangkok................................8
   Introduction to Bangkok... 8
   Why Should you Visit Bangkok?............................. 11
   Best Time to Visit... 13
   How to Get There... 17
   Important Tips for First-Time Visitors...................... 21
Chapter 2: Planning Your Trip to Bangkok...............26
   Preparing for Your Trip...26
   Budgeting for Bangkok.. 29
   Accommodation Options..33
   Getting Around The City.. 43
   Safety & Health..47
Chapter 3: Exploring Bangkok's Attractions........... 52
   Top Tourist Attractions.. 52
   Hidden Gems in Bangkok.. 59
   Shopping in Bangkok...65
   Cultural and Historical Sites....................................69
   Outdoor Activities and Parks................................... 73
Chapter 4: Experiencing Bangkok's Cuisine........... 76

Introduction to Thai Cuisine................................... 76
Street Food.. 79
Best Restaurants in Bangkok................................ 87
Night Markets and Food Festivals......................... 94
Traditional Thai Dining Etiquette............................98
Chapter 5: Bangkok's Vibrant Nightlife.................. 102
Rooftop Bars and Nightclubs................................ 102
Cultural Nightlife... 111
Bangkok's Entertainment Districts........................ 113
Night Markets and Evening Experiences............. 118
Relaxing and Unwinding....................................... 123
Chapter 6: Shopping in Bangkok............................132
Markets to Visit... 132
Modern Malls.. 142
Unique Souvenirs and Gifts.................................. 146
Haggling Tips.. 148
Fashion & Design... 152
Chapter 7: Day Trips and Nearby Destinations......156
Ayutthaya.. 157
Kanchanaburi..164
Pattaya..170
Damnoen Saduak Floating Market....................... 173
Nakhon Pathom.. 176
Chapter 8: Practical Information for Visitors......... 179
Emergency Numbers and Contact Information..... 179

Currency & Banking... 181
Language & Communication............................... 185
Internet and SIM Cards... 189
Public Holidays and Festivals............................... 192
Chapter 9: Suggested Itinerary for Bangkok......... 198
3-Day Itinerary for First-Time Visitors................... 198
7-Day Itinerary for a Deeper Exploration of Bangkok. 202
Conclusion.. 205

MAP OF BANGKOK

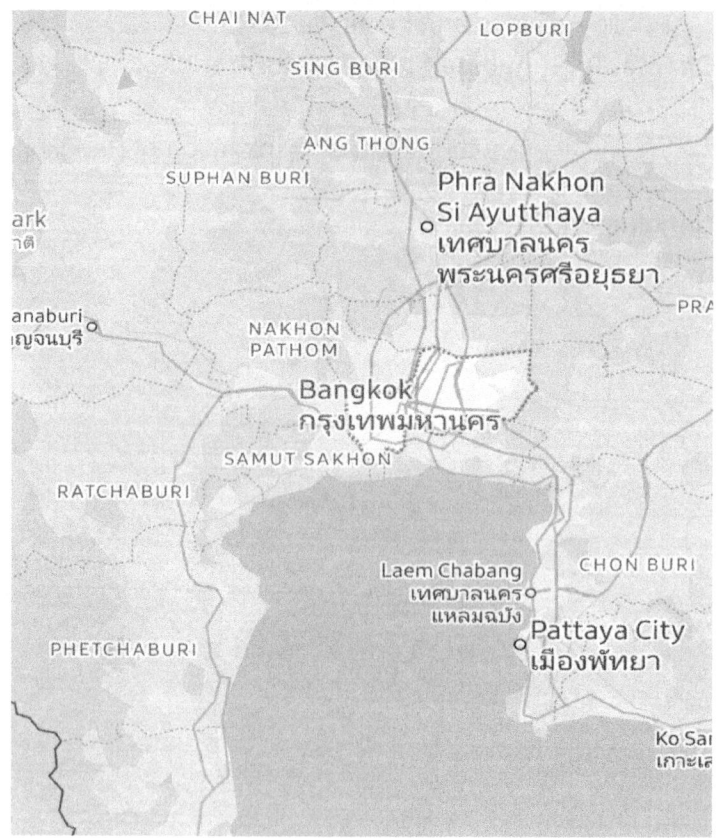

Chapter 1: Welcome to Bangkok

Introduction to Bangkok

Welcome to Bangkok, a city that never ceases to amaze me, no matter how frequently I visit. It's a city where ancient traditions combine harmoniously with modern life, resulting in an intoxicating and unique atmosphere.

Bangkok is Thailand's pulsating heart, a cultural and economic powerhouse that has evolved from its humble origins as a little trade port in the 15th century. Today, it is a huge metropolis of more than 11 million people, famed for its bustling streets, beautiful temples, and a lifestyle that combines hustle with harmony.

Bangkok has a rich cultural heritage. It is home to approximately 400 temples, each one a work of delicate craftsmanship with profound spiritual importance. Wat Phra Kaew, located on the grounds of the Grand Palace, is the crown jewel—a sacred place that holds the Emerald Buddha, one of Thailand's most cherished symbols. However, the city's cultural wealth extends beyond its temples. It can be found in bustling street markets, the rhythm of traditional Thai music, and even the way people greet one another with a warm grin and a "wai."

Bangkok serves as Thailand's economic powerhouse. It is a global commercial hub, with towering towers housing multinational firms and cutting-edge startups. The city's skyline reflects its economic development—modern, ambitious, and ever-changing. Nonetheless, amidst the growth, Bangkok keeps its spirit, as evidenced by the modest enterprises and family-run markets that coexist with luxury retail centers.

Bangkok's history is intriguing. It formally became the capital in 1782, when King Rama I established it as the seat of the Chakri dynasty, which continues to rule today. Warfare, commerce growth, and cultural revolutions have all contributed to the city's current status as a dynamic destination. Walking across Bangkok is like reading through a history book, with each district conveying its own story—from Rattanakosin's royal legacy to Chinatown's lively multiculturalism.

What interests me the most about Bangkok is how it welcomes paradoxes. It's a country where ancient traditions coexist with modern goals, where the sound of monks chanting blends with the hum of traffic, and where you can eat a street-side bowl of noodles in the shadow of a luxury skyscraper. These differences are what give Bangkok its vibrancy and compelling appeal.

Why Should you Visit Bangkok?

Let me explain why Bangkok holds such a particular place in my heart and should be on your travel bucket list. Bangkok is more than just a city; it is an experience, dynamic and full of surprises around every corner. The vibrancy in this bustling city is palpable from the moment you arrive. It is a city where the antique and modern coexist in perfect harmony, resulting in a lively and stimulating atmosphere unlike any other.

A Feast for the Senses

Bangkok is a sensory overload, in the greatest way. Consider walking through vibrant street markets, where the aroma of sizzling street food fills the air. Imagine yourself surrounded by golden temple towers that gleam in the sun, while the rhythmic chanting of monks provides a moment of peace despite the bustle. Whether it's the bustling alleyways of Chinatown or the tranquility of a temple courtyard, Bangkok keeps your senses stimulated.

The Cultural Melting Pot

What I admire most about Bangkok is how it honors its rich history while embracing modernity. You may see the breathtaking Grand Palace and Wat Phra Kaew, which represent centuries of history and artistry. Then, the same day, you may be drinking drinks at a rooftop bar with breathtaking views of the city skyline. Bangkok's blend of old and new is seamless—it's a city that values its heritage while confidently moving forward.

Street Food Paradise
Bangkok is a foodie's dream come true. The city is world-renowned for its street cuisine, and it meets up to the expectations. I can't recall how many nights I've spent trying fiery bowls of Tom Yum, smokey Pad Thai, and sweet mango sticky rice from local sellers. Each meal is a work of art, made right in front of you and bursting with flavors that dance on your tongue. And the best part? It is reasonably priced, so you may eat to your heart's delight without breaking the wallet.

Endless Adventures

Bangkok never gets boring—there's always something fresh to discover. You can take a traditional long-tail boat to explore the city's klongs (canals) or enter the maze-like Chatuchak Market, one of the world's largest. One of my favorite hobbies is riding a tuk-tuk through the bustling streets at night, with neon lights flashing by and the hum of the city all around.

A City of Warmth and Smiles
Finally, the people of Bangkok make it genuinely unforgettable. Thailand, sometimes known as the "Land of Smiles," lives up to its reputation. Everywhere I went in Bangkok, I was greeted with friendliness and real affection. Whether it's a vendor in a market or a stranger directing you, the locals make you feel welcome and at ease.

Best Time to Visit

When arranging a trip to Bangkok, scheduling is crucial. The city's tropical environment can be severe, with hot, humid days followed by brief rain showers, but knowing when to visit can make a big difference in your experience. Over the years, I've discovered that the best time to visit is entirely dependent on your choices, whether you want to escape the heat, attend festivals, or see the city at its most active.

Seasonal Weather Patterns
Bangkok has three distinct seasons, each providing a unique atmosphere for visitors:

Hot Season (March-June)
This is the hottest period of the year, with temperatures exceeding 35°C (95°F). While it may be uncomfortable for some, it is also the low season for tourism, resulting in fewer crowds and lower accommodation costs. If you're prepared for the heat and prefer quieter surroundings, now might be the best time to explore the city.

Rainy Season (July-October)
Expect heavy rain, particularly in the afternoons and evenings. It's a humid, damp period, but the rain can help to cool things off. Don't let it discourage you; the city still has a lot to offer. Furthermore, there will be fewer tourists, and the city's rich nature will be stunning. If you can

withstand the rain, now is the time to get the greatest accommodation deals and visit calmer sights.

Cool Season (November–February)
Personally, this is my preferred time to visit Bangkok. The weather is significantly more pleasant, with temperatures ranging from 20°C (68°F) to 30°C (86°F). The humidity level reduces, making it ideal for visiting the city's outdoor attractions, marketplaces, and temples. This is peak season, so expect more tourists, but the mood is celebratory and colorful. It also coincides with Bangkok's famed festivals, making it an exciting time to visit.

Festivals and Cultural Events
Bangkok is famed for its stunning festivals, which often coincide with the cooler months. If you're interested in experiencing local culture, these festivals are essential:

Songkran (April)
The Thai New Year, which takes place in mid-April, is a city-wide water fight and one of Bangkok's most

well-known festivities. Locals and tourists alike take to the streets with water cannons, splashing everyone they see. If you're willing to get messy, it's a fun and memorable experience.

Loy Krathong (November)
This celebration, held in November, involves people gathering along rivers to release miniature, flower-filled boats (krathongs) into the water. The sight of thousands of illuminated boats gliding down the Chao Phraya River is nothing short of spectacular. It's a stunning cultural festival that I wholeheartedly endorse.

Chinese New Year (January/February)
This event brings Bangkok's Chinatown to life, with dragon dances, street entertainment, and food vendors filling the streets. The excitement is contagious, and now is an excellent time to witness the city's mix of Thai and Chinese cultures.

How to Get There

When planning a trip to Bangkok, one of the first things to think about is how to get there, and thankfully, the city is well connected to the rest of the world. Whether you're flying in from a nearby country or from around the world, Bangkok's two main airports, Suvarnabhumi Airport (BKK) and Don Mueang International Airport (DMK), offer a choice of ways to get to the city core.

International Flights
Bangkok is a significant international hub, having direct flights to and from places all around the globe. Thai Airways, Singapore Airlines, and Emirates operate regular flights into Bangkok, and budget airlines such as AirAsia and Scoot provide economical connections to neighboring nations and beyond. Whether you're going from Europe, Asia, or the Americas, you'll most likely find a direct trip to Bangkok, which takes about 10-13 hours from major Western cities such as New York or London.

Transportation Options From the Airport

Once you arrive, getting to your hotel or the city center is reasonably simple, with various efficient transportation alternatives.

Airport Railway Link (ARL)
If you want a quick and inexpensive method to travel into the city, the Airport Rail Link is your best option. The train travels from Suvarnabhumi Airport to the city center, stopping at strategic areas like Phaya Thai Station, where you can easily connect to the BTS Skytrain. The trip takes around 30 minutes and costs between 45 and 90 THB ($1.5 to $3 USD), depending on where you get off.

Taxis
Taxis are readily available at both airports, and while they provide door-to-door service, keep in mind that Bangkok traffic can be congested, so travel times may vary. Taxis from Suvarnabhumi to central Bangkok (such as Sukhumvit or Silom) normally cost between 300 and 500 THB ($9 and $15 USD), including airport fees and tolls. To avoid overcharging, always request that the meter be used.

Airport Shuttle Bus

If you're staying in a more affordable region or don't mind taking a slower but cheaper route, the shuttle buses at Suvarnabhumi Airport are an excellent choice. These buses travel to major destinations including Khao San Road, Siam Square, and Silom. The fee is fairly low, around 30-50 THB ($1 USD), but the trip can take an hour or more, depending on traffic.

Private Transfers

For those who prefer a more pleasant and hassle-free experience, you can pre-book a private transfer from the airport to your hotel. This can be especially useful if you're traveling in a group or have a lot of luggage. Many firms provide services from both Suvarnabhumi and Don Mueang, with fees ranging from 600-1000 THB ($18-$30 USD) for one-way travel, depending on your destination in the city.

Don Muang Airport

If you're flying into Don Mueang, which mostly serves budget carriers such as Nok Air, AirAsia, and Thai Lion Air, your transportation options are similar. Taxis are accessible, and the cost of getting to the city center ranges between 200 and 400 THB ($6 and $12 USD). Alternatively, take the A1 bus to Mo Chit Station, which is connected to the BTS Skytrain.

Tips for a Smooth Arrival

Avoid Rush Hour
Bangkok traffic may be chaotic, especially during the morning (7-9 AM) and evening (4-7 PM) rush hours. If possible, schedule your arrival outside of these busy periods to avoid being trapped in traffic for too long.

SIM Cards
Upon arrival, you may easily acquire a SIM card at the airport for internet access and phone calls, making your stay in Bangkok much more manageable.

Currency
While ATMs are available at both airports, you may want to exchange a small amount of currency

before leaving in case you require cash right away upon arrival.

Important Tips for First-Time Visitors

If you're planning your first vacation to Bangkok, prepare for an incredible adventure! This bustling city combines ancient traditions with modern wonders, and knowing a few basics can help your visit go more smoothly. Here are my top suggestions for traversing the city with ease.

Currency and Money Matters
When you arrive in Bangkok, you will use Thai Baht (THB) as your money. ATMs are widely available throughout the city, and most accept international cards; nonetheless, it is usually a good idea to carry extra cash for smaller transactions, particularly in markets or with street vendors. You can exchange money at the airport or in local exchange businesses at competitive rates.

While credit cards are frequently accepted in hotels, restaurants, and stores in prominent tourist destinations, some establishments, particularly markets or tiny shops, only accept cash. Don't forget to notify your bank that you will be traveling so that your card works properly abroad.

Language
Thai is Bangkok's official language, but don't worry—many people working in the tourism business speak English, particularly in popular tourist destinations. However, knowing a few simple phrases can go a long way and will be appreciated by the locals. Here are some useful phrases.

• Hello, Sawasdee (pronounced sah-wah-dee).

• Thank you: Khob khun (pronounced kop koon).

• Yes, Chai (pronounced chai).

• No, Mai (pronounced me).

• What amount? - Tao Rai? (pronounced: tao rai).

Even if many individuals understand English, utilizing these basic phrases can demonstrate respect for the culture and can result in warmer treatment.

Etiquette and Cultural Norms
Thailand has a rich cultural background, and while it is a hospitable country for tourists, you should be mindful of the following cultural conventions and etiquette:

Respect to the King
The Thai royal family is highly esteemed, and any disrespect to them is handled extremely seriously. Portraits of the king are commonly found around the city, particularly in government buildings. It is crucial to show respect, so refrain from making jokes or casual remarks about the monarchy.

Temple Etiquette
When visiting temples (or watts), please dress modestly. This includes protecting your shoulders and knees; no shorts or sleeveless tops. It is also usual to take off your shoes before visiting religious buildings, so wear socks or clean feet!

The Wai

The traditional Thai welcome involves pressing your palms together in a prayer-like attitude and bowing slightly. While it is not required to return the wai (particularly with strangers), it is a nice way to show respect. If someone offers you a wai, it is customary to return it with a little bow, but if you are hesitant, a simple smile and nod would suffice.

Head and Feet
In Thai tradition, the head is the most important part of the body, and the feet are the least sacred. Avoid touching anyone's head and never aim your foot at people, statues, or religious representations, especially in temples.

Safety Basics in Bangkok
Bangkok is generally a secure place for tourists, but like with any large city, you should stay alert of your surroundings and take simple measures. Here are some safety tips that I follow on my trips:

Traffic and Pedestrian Safety
Traffic in Bangkok may be chaotic, and it is not uncommon for motorists to run red lights. Use pedestrian bridges or crosswalks wherever

available, and be extra cautious when crossing streets, even if the light is green. If you're taking public transportation, especially tuk-tuks, always agree on the fee before beginning your journey.

Avoid Scams
Bangkok is a renowned tourist destination, which has led to a number of frauds targeting visitors. One classic scam is a tuk-tuk or taxi driver giving a tour at a "special" low price, which frequently leads to a visit to pricey stores. To minimize surprises, always confirm fares in advance or utilize ride-hailing applications such as Grab.

Keep your Belongings Secure
Petty theft, such as pickpocketing, can occur, particularly in busy settings or markets. Always keep an eye on your stuff, wear a money belt, and keep valuables in your front pockets.

Emergency Numbers
It's a good idea to know the local emergency contact information just in case. For general emergencies, dial 191. To contact tourist police, phone 1155.

Chapter 2: Planning Your Trip to Bangkok

Preparing for Your Trip

Planning a trip to Bangkok is thrilling, but it's also critical to cover all the bases before you leave. Allow me to lead you through the entire preparation process, from visa requirements to health suggestions and what to carry.

Visa Requirements
Before you board your aircraft, determine whether you require a visa to visit Thailand. Thailand allows numerous nations to enter without a visa for up to 30 days. If you intend to stay for an extended period of time, you may require a tourist visa, which you can obtain at your local Thai embassy or consulate. Some passengers can also get a visa on arrival, but make sure your country qualifies.

For those considering an extended stay of a few months or more, consider the Special Tourist Visa (STV) or other long-term visa options, such as the Thailand Elite Visa or education visas. Make sure your passport is valid for at least six months from the date of entrance, and keep a copy of your travel documents on hand just in case.

Health Tips
Now let's speak about how to keep healthy while exploring Bangkok. It is a good idea to consult with your doctor about any immunizations you may require. Common ones include Hepatitis A, Typhoid, and Tetanus. Dengue fever is common in tropical places, so bring insect repellent and wear

light, long-sleeved clothing if you plan on spending a lot of time outside.

The city is largely safe, although I always advocate drinking bottled water rather than tap water to avoid stomach upset. Bangkok's heat can be harsh, especially if you are not used to tropical conditions, so remain hydrated and take frequent breaks from the sun. Don't forget to bring some basic drugs, such as anti-diarrhea tablets and pain painkillers, just in case.

What to Pack?
Packing for Bangkok is rather simple, but there are a few essential items that will make your trip go much more smoothly. The city's temperature is hot and humid all year, so wear lightweight, breathable clothing. However, if you wish to visit temples, you must dress modestly. Consider wearing long skirts or slacks with tops that hide your shoulders.

Comfortable shoes are an essential! Believe me, you'll be walking a lot, particularly in markets, temples, and parks. A good pair of sandals or sneakers will protect your feet.

Do not Forget these Essentials

• **A portable charger:** With all the images you'll take and maps you'll look up, your phone's battery will quickly drop.

• **A reusable water bottle:** Many hotels and cafes include water refill stations, which assist to reduce plastic waste.

• **An adapter:** Thailand utilizes type C and F plugs with a voltage of 220 V. If your gadgets utilize a different type of plug, you will need an adaptor.

Budgeting for Bangkok

When I originally started arranging my trip to Bangkok, I was surprised by how affordable the city might be, depending on your travel preferences. Whether you're a traveler on a limited budget or searching for inexpensive luxury, Bangkok has something for you. Here's a summary of how much you should expect to spend, as well as some money-saving ideas.

Suggested Daily Budget

Budget Travelers
With street food, hostels, and public transportation, a daily budget of ฿1,000-฿1,500 (about $30-$40) is plenty.

Mid-Range Travelers
around additional comfort, such as dining in casual restaurants, staying in inexpensive hotels, and mixing public transport with Grab rides, aim around ฿2,500-฿3,500 (about $70-$100) every day.

Luxury Travelers
Staying in high-end hotels, dining at upmarket restaurants, and booking private tours can cost up to ฿6,000 (about $170) every day.

Cost-cutting Tips

Embrace Street Food
Street food is not only tasty, but also extremely economical. You may discover delicious foods like

Pad Thai, Som Tum (papaya salad), and grilled skewers for as little as ฿40-฿80 ($1-$2). Chinatown (Yaowarat) and the street booths near Sukhumvit are two excellent options for street cuisine.

Use Public Transportation
Bangkok's BTS Skytrain and MRT subway are quick, reliable, and inexpensive. A single ride costs ฿16-฿59 ($0.50-$1.50) based on distance, while a day pass for unlimited rides costs ฿140 ($4). To save time and money, avoid taking cabs during high traffic hours.

Shop at Local Markets
Instead of shopping at expensive malls, visit Chatuchak Weekend Market or Pratunam Market for low-cost souvenirs, clothing, and accessories. Don't forget to haggle; it's expected!

Choose Free or low-cost Attractions
While the Grand Palace and Wat Phra Kaew have entrance fees, several smaller temples like Wat Arun or Wat Saket (Golden Mount) levy minor fees (about ฿50-฿100, $1.50-$3). Free parks such as

Lumpini and Benjakitti provide a calm getaway from the hustle and bustle of the city.

Stay in Budget Accommodations
Bangkok's hostels and cheap hotels provide clean and comfortable lodgings starting from ฿300-฿600 ($8-$15)/night. Look for long-term stay savings on platforms such as Agoda or Booking.com.

Money Saving Advice

Carry Small Bills
Street vendors rarely have change for high sums, so carry small notes and coins on hand.

Use Cash Wisely
While larger restaurants accept credit cards, the majority of street sellers and small businesses accept cash only.

Avoid Currency Exchange Traps
To get better rates, exchange your money at recognized locations such as SuperRich or other licensed booths rather than the airport.

Download Travel Apps
Apps like Grab (for rides), Eatigo (for dining discounts), and Klook (for activity bargains) can help you save a lot of money.

Plan ahead for SIM Cards
To avoid costly roaming charges, purchase a prepaid tourist SIM with unlimited data for approximately ฿299-฿599 ($8-$17).

Accommodation Options

When I first arrived in Bangkok, I was astounded by the sheer number of places to stay. Whether you want to splurge on luxury, keep to a mid-range budget, or save money with low-cost options, Bangkok has something for everyone. Here's what I've learned from my time investigating the city's lodging options.

Luxury Hotels
If you want a sumptuous experience, Bangkok's luxury hotels will not disappoint. The city is home to world-renowned enterprises that provide

first-rate amenities, beautiful views, and exceptional service.

Mandarin Oriental Bangkok

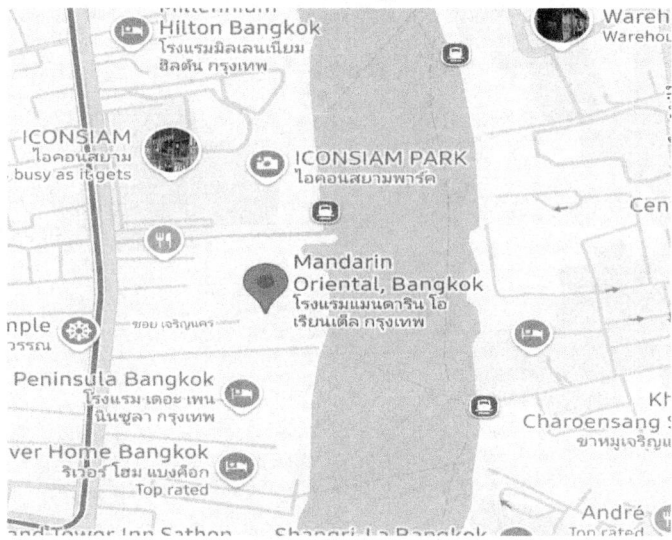

This iconic hotel on the Chao Phraya River is a true jewel. The rooms combine modern luxury with traditional Thai décor, and the riverbank dining experience is remarkable.

The Peninsula Bangkok

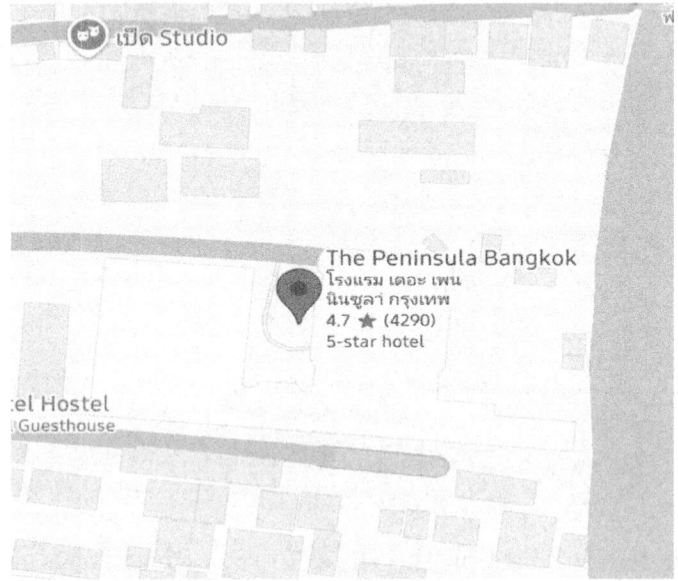

Staying here seems like escaping the city's hustle. The river views, infinity pool, and calm setting make it well worth the money.

Siam Kempinski Hotel

If you enjoy shopping, this one is a dream come true—it's directly adjacent to Siam Paragon. The beautiful garden pools and elegant rooms provide an ideal combination of relaxation and convenience.

Mid-Range Options

Bangkok features many mid-range hotels that do not sacrifice quality for visitors seeking a blend of comfort and cost.

Chatrium Hotel Riverside

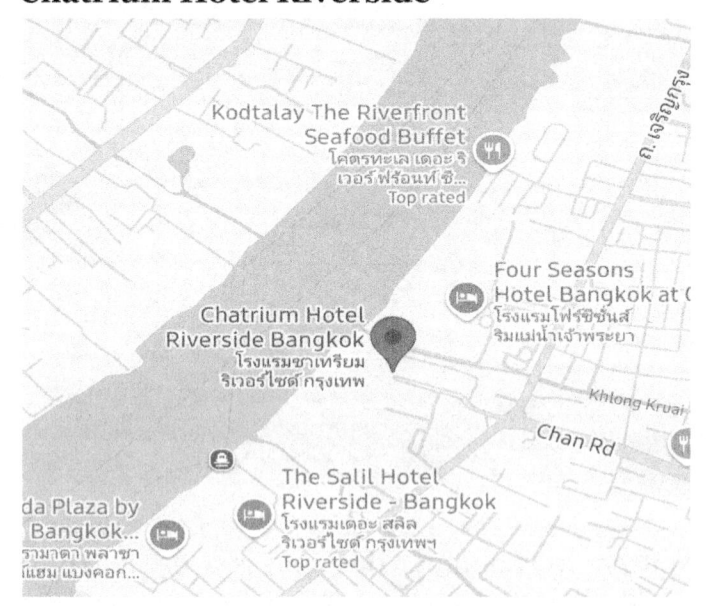

I stayed here on one occasion, and the river views were breathtaking. It provides big rooms and excellent eating alternatives without breaking the wallet.

Amara Bangkok

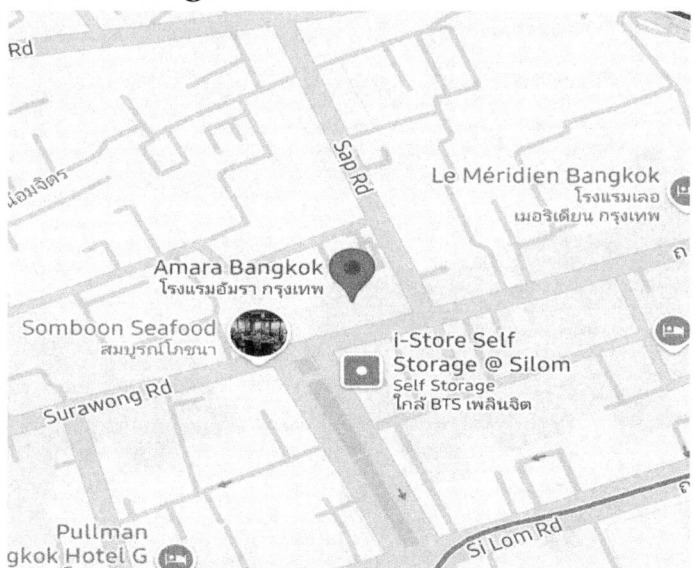

This hotel, located in the city center, is ideal for exploring neighborhoods such as Silom and Chinatown. The rooftop pool is the highlight!

Adelphi Forty Nine

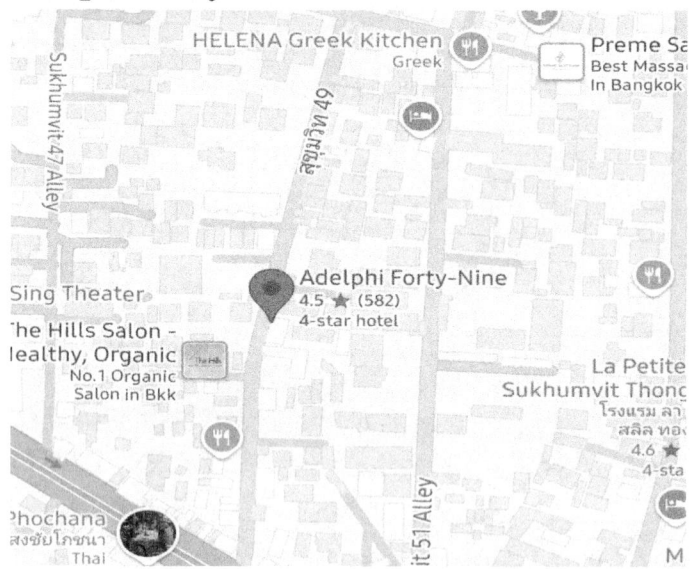

Tucked away in a quieter neighborhood, this hotel provides a friendly atmosphere with big rooms and easy access to fashionable cafés in Thonglor.

Budget-Friendly Hostels

Traveling on a budget? Don't worry—Bangkok is one of the greatest cities for economical, clean, and comfy accommodations. Hostels here aren't just about saving money; many have a terrific social ambiance that's ideal for meeting other travelers.

Lub D Bangkok Siam

I've recommended this hostel numerous times. It is conveniently located near the BTS Skytrain station and the MBK and Siam shopping areas.

The Yard Hostel

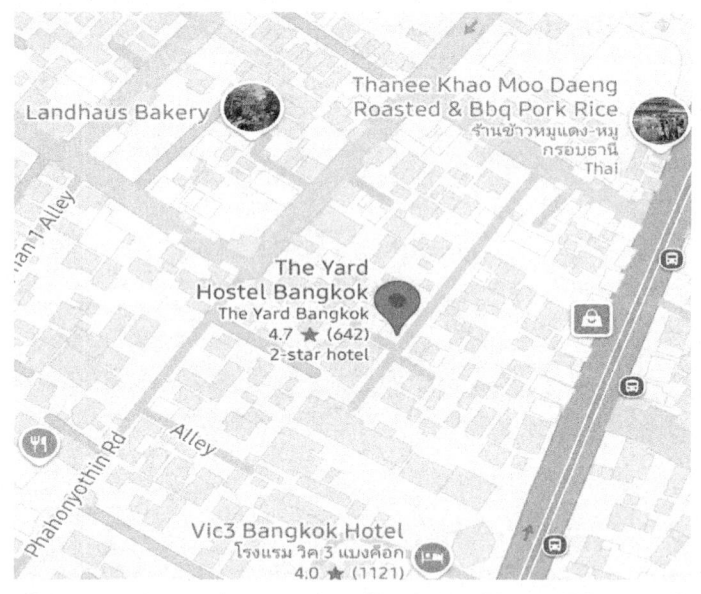

This one is environmentally friendly and located in Ari, one of Bangkok's nicest areas. The garden area is ideal for unwinding after a busy day of exploration.

Niras Bankoc Cultural Hostel

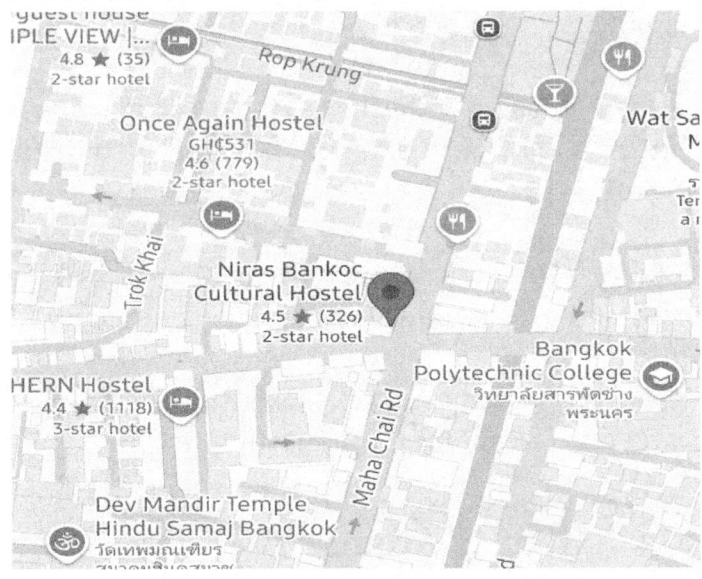

It's conveniently located near the Old Town, making it ideal for those looking to visit temples and cultural attractions. The vintage-style decor is a lovely addition.

Tips for Selecting the Right Area

Choosing the ideal place to stay in Bangkok relies on your priorities.

• Sukhumvit is ideal for nightlife, restaurants, and shopping.

• Silom: Ideal for business tourists and those seeking a balance of modern and traditional Bangkok.

• Riverside: Ideal for individuals seeking breathtaking vistas and a more relaxing ambiance.

• Khao San Road: A backpacker's paradise with several hostels and low-cost guesthouses.

Getting Around The City

Navigating Bangkok can appear daunting at first, but once you get the hang of it, you'll discover that it's actually quite simple. The city boasts a great and diverse transportation system that accommodates all types of travelers. Whether you're visiting the historic temples or shopping at the bustling markets, here's how I get around this dynamic city.

SkyTrain (BTS)
The Skytrain, or BTS, is one of the greatest ways to get around the city, especially during peak hours when traffic can be a nightmare. It's quick and efficient, and the stations are located close to large shopping malls, marketplaces, and prominent tourist attractions. I enjoy traveling the Sukhumvit Line since it provides easy access to destinations including Siam Square, Mo Chit, and Chatuchak Market. Tickets are reasonably priced, and the trains are air-conditioned, making it a comfortable option in Bangkok's heat. Plus, there are clear signage in both Thai and English, making it simple to figure out.

MRT (underground)
If you're going to regions that the Skytrain doesn't go to, such as Chinatown or the vibrant districts near the river, the MRT (Metro) is an excellent alternative. It is not as comprehensive as the BTS, but it does provide easy access to famous areas. The MRT stations are easily accessible and run similarly

to the Skytrain, with clear signage and well-maintained amenities. I also like how it connects straight to the airport via the Airport Link line, which is convenient if you're visiting or departing the city.

Tuk-Tuks
No vacation to Bangkok is complete without riding in a tuk-tuk! These small three-wheeled vehicles are iconic and provide a pleasant, if slightly chaotic, experience. You'll typically see them flying about crowded locations like Khao San Road or around key tourist sites. Tuk-tuks are ideal for short trips and provide a unique way to explore the streets, but be sure to agree on a price before getting in to avoid being overcharged. I usually enjoy the rush of zipping through the crowded streets, but be prepared for the heat and loudness!

Boats
Bangkok's water transit is another fantastic way to move around, as the Chao Phraya River runs through the city. The public boat service is quick and provides a picturesque and pleasant way to travel, particularly if you're visiting Wat Arun or the

Grand Palace. There are several sorts of boats, ranging from express boats to slower ferries, and they are an excellent method to avoid the city's renowned traffic congestion. Furthermore, the river views are breathtaking, making it a consistently enjoyable experience.

Taxis

Taxis are widely available around Bangkok, making them a practical option whether you're traveling with luggage or going somewhere off the usual route. When taking a taxi, be sure the driver uses the meter, as many drivers will try to provide a flat charge that is significantly greater than the metered fare. Taxis are trustworthy in my experience, however it may take some time to flag one down during rush hour owing to traffic. To minimize confusion, have your destination written in Thai (your hotel can assist you with this).

Grab (Ride-hailing)

Grab, Southeast Asia's version of Uber, is another excellent option for getting about Bangkok. It's quite convenient for both short and long travels, and you may pay with a credit card or cash. I appreciate how simple it is to book a ride through the app, and you can follow your driver so you never have to wonder where they are. Grab cabs and Grab bikes are also available, providing greater flexibility based on the time of day and traffic circumstances.

Safety & Health

When visiting Bangkok, it is critical to keep aware about health and safety rules to ensure a worry-free time. While the city is typically safe, I recommend taking a few steps to make your stay here more pleasurable and secure.

Health Precautions

Vaccinations
Before traveling to Bangkok, make sure you have all of your normal immunizations, including measles, mumps, rubella (MMR), and tetanus. Additionally, it's a good idea to talk with your healthcare provider about immunizations for diseases like Hepatitis A, Hepatitis B, and typhoid, especially if you intend to travel to rural areas or consume street food.

Mosquito Protection

Bangkok has a tropical climate, thus mosquitoes are a typical worry. Dengue fever and the Zika virus are both present in the region, thus precautions must be taken. If you're staying in a less urban setting, I recommend wearing long sleeves, applying DEET-based mosquito repellent, and sleeping under a mosquito net.

Drinking Water

When I visit Bangkok, I always drink bottled water. The tap water in the city is not deemed safe to drink, so avoid using it for anything more than brushing your teeth. Staying hydrated will be easy because bottled water is readily available practically everywhere.

Street Food Safety

Bangkok is well-known for its amazing street food, and I highly recommend that you taste some! However, be mindful of where and what you eat. Look for vendors who have a high client turnover and serve cuisine that is freshly cooked in front of you. This decreases the possibilities of ingesting food that has been sitting out for too long.

Safety Tips

Traffic Safety
Bangkok's traffic might be overpowering, therefore I recommend remaining attentive while crossing the street. Thai drivers frequently do not obey pedestrian signals, therefore always look both ways and use pedestrian bridges or crosswalks whenever available. If you're using a tuk-tuk or a taxi, make sure to agree on the fee before beginning your journey, or utilize a metered cab.

Pickpockets and Scams
While Bangkok is a relatively safe city, petty theft and frauds sometimes occur, particularly in tourist-heavy areas such as Khao San Road and Chatuchak Market. Keep your stuff nearby, and I recommend utilizing a money belt or a lockable bag with a zipper. Be careful of anyone promoting "too good to be true" deals, particularly around popular tourist attractions.

Safe at Night
I adore Bangkok's bustling nightlife, but I always take additional precautions after dark. Stay in well-lit, busy locations, and avoid wandering alone late at night in unknown districts. If you're out late, I recommend using a reputable ride-sharing service like Grab rather than grabbing a taxi on the street.

Emergency Numbers
It's always reassuring to know who to contact in an emergency. Here are the main emergency contacts in Bangkok:

• Police: 191.

• Ambulance and Medical Assistance (1554)

• Tourist Police Number: 1155 (English-speaking staff available)

• Fire Department: 199.

Healthcare in Bangkok

Hospital and Clinics

Bangkok has an excellent healthcare system, and the city is home to several high-quality international hospitals, like Bumrungrad International Hospital and Samitivej Sukhumvit Hospital, which specialize in catering to foreign tourists. Many clinics in the city provide economical treatments for minor diseases or basic care. I usually recommend purchasing travel insurance that includes medical coverage just in case.

Pharmacies
Pharmacies are easily accessible across the city, and many are open 24 hours a day, seven days a week. Over-the-counter drugs are available for common travel diseases such as stomach difficulties, headaches, and allergies. Just keep in mind that prescription drugs require a doctor's note or a visit to a local clinic.

Chapter 3: Exploring Bangkok's Attractions

Top Tourist Attractions

As soon as I stepped into the center of Bangkok, I was struck by the city's distinct blend of history, culture, and modern vibrancy. Among the major attractions, I was repeatedly drawn to the city's renowned temples and grand architecture. Here's a list of must-see sights that I strongly suggest for any traveler.

The Grand Palace

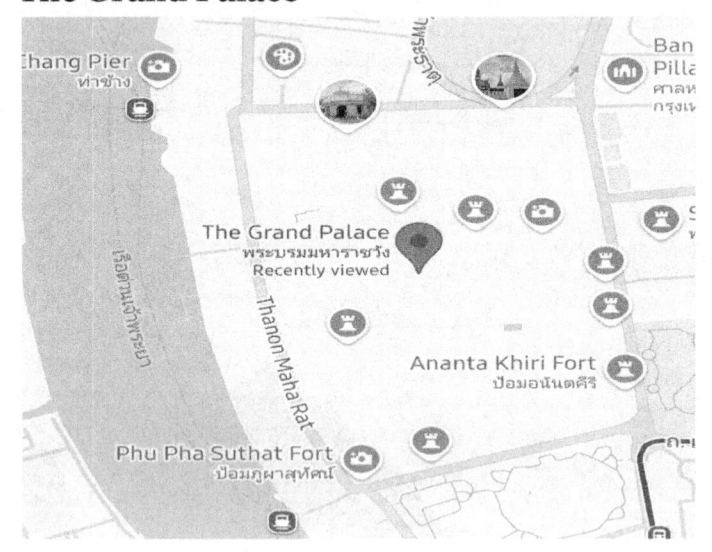

The Grand Palace is one of Bangkok's most magnificent monuments and a must-see. This complex of glittering buildings was formerly the royal residence for Thai kings and is now a reminder of Thailand's grandeur and past. The beautiful architecture, complete with golden spires and spacious courtyards, left me dumbfounded.

The palace is home to several important structures, notably the Chakri Mahaprasad Hall and the Emerald Buddha shrine (Wat Phra Kaew), Thailand's most sacred shrine. It's a place where you can really feel appreciation for Thai culture. As a demonstration of respect, visitors should dress modestly—no shorts or sleeveless tops.

Wat Phra Kaew (The Temple of the Emerald Buddha)

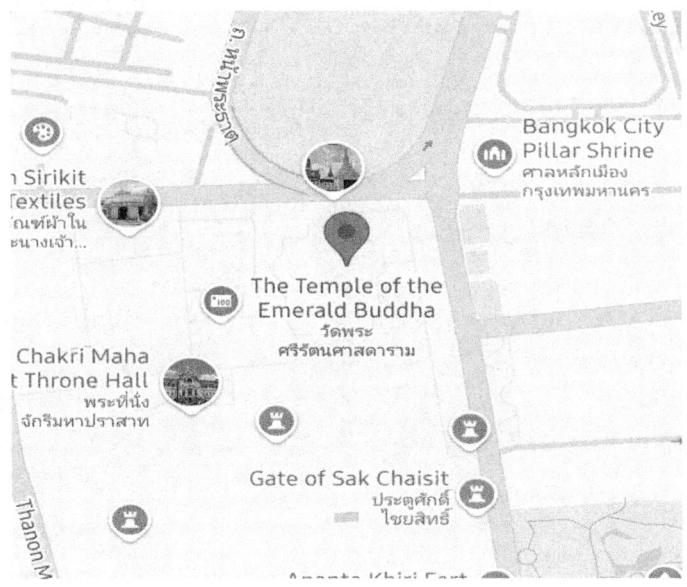

Wat Phra Kaew, located near to the Grand Palace, is more than just a temple; it is also a cultural asset. The Emerald Buddha, Thailand's most renowned religious artifact, is kept here. The temple's breathtaking architecture, with its golden chedis (stupas) and exquisite murals illustrating Thai mythology, captivated me. Visitors from all over the world pay their respects and admire the temple's beauty.

Wat Arun (The Temple of Dawn)

Wat Arun, located across the Chao Phraya River from the Grand Palace, is one of Bangkok's most renowned sites. The temple's lofty spire, or prang, is coated in fine porcelain tiles and shines in the sunlight. It is especially beautiful at sunset. I arrived by boat along the river, and the view of Wat Arun from the water was really breathtaking. If you're prepared for a challenge, I recommend climbing the steep steps for panoramic views of the river and city.

Other Notable Temples
While the Grand Palace, Wat Phra Kaew, and Wat Arun are the primary attractions, Bangkok has numerous other wonderful temples that are well worth visiting:

Wat Pho (Temple of Reclining Buddha)

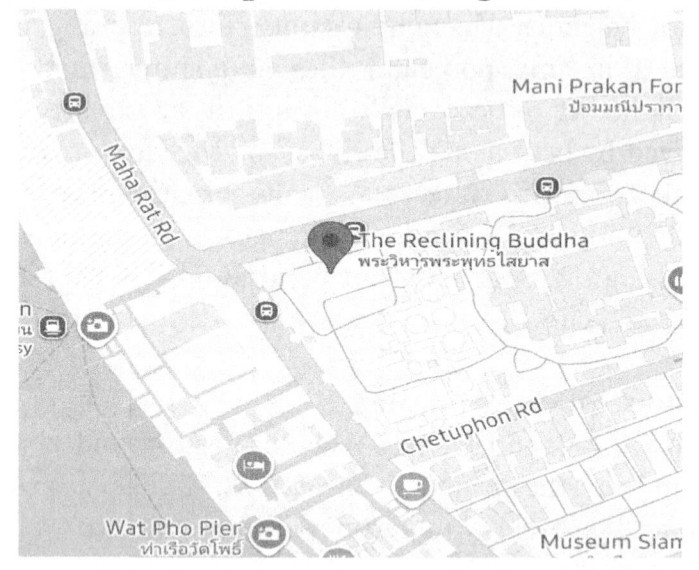

Wat Pho, located a short walk from the Grand Palace, is home to the famed Reclining Buddha, a 46-meter-long monument. I couldn't stroll by without admiring its sheer immensity and golden magnificence.

Wat Saket (Golden Mountain)

This lesser-known gem provides a tranquil respite from the city's hustle and bustle. I went to the summit for a peaceful view of Bangkok's skyline, with the golden stupa gleaming in the sun.

Temple of the Golden Buddha (Wat Traimit)

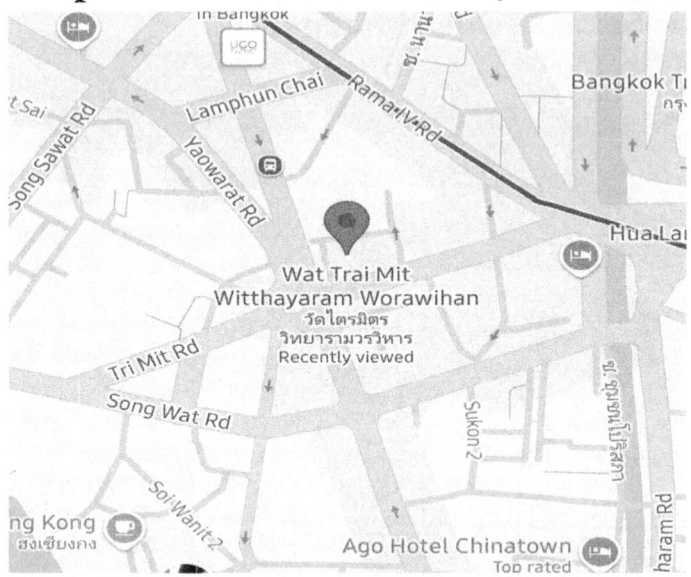

This temple, which houses the world's largest solid gold Buddha statue, represents Thailand's rich cultural and spiritual tradition.

Hidden Gems in Bangkok

Bangkok is famous for its bright streets, dazzling temples, and renowned buildings, but as I traveled the city, I discovered a few hidden treasures that provide a quieter, more real side to this frenetic metropolis. If you want to avoid the throng and see Bangkok as a native, these lesser-known sites will show you the city's true appeal. Here are some of my favorite discoveries.

Lesser-known Temples
While the Grand Palace and Wat Arun receive most of the attention, Bangkok also has other lovely temples that go unnoticed yet are just as enchanting.

Wat Ratchanatdaram

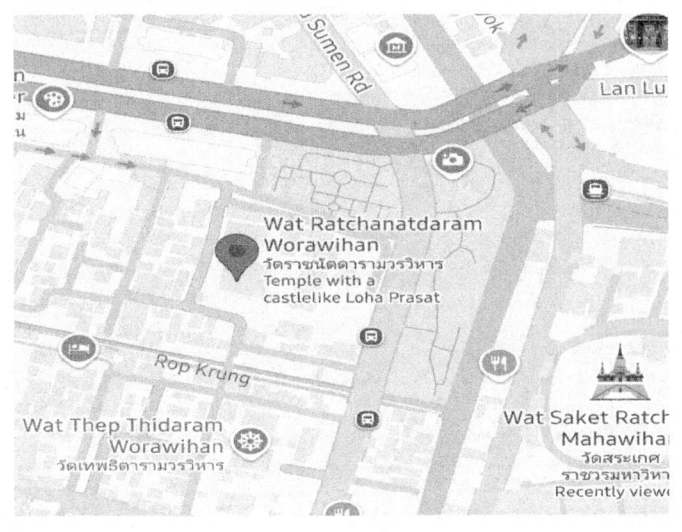

Wat Ratchanatdaram, tucked away in the ancient town, is a magnificent but often missed temple. Its golden Loha Prasat (Metal Castle) is unique in the world and a testament to historic Thai architecture. I enjoy arriving here early in the morning, when the sun shines off the golden spires, providing a peaceful scene away from the rush and bustle.

Wat Suthat

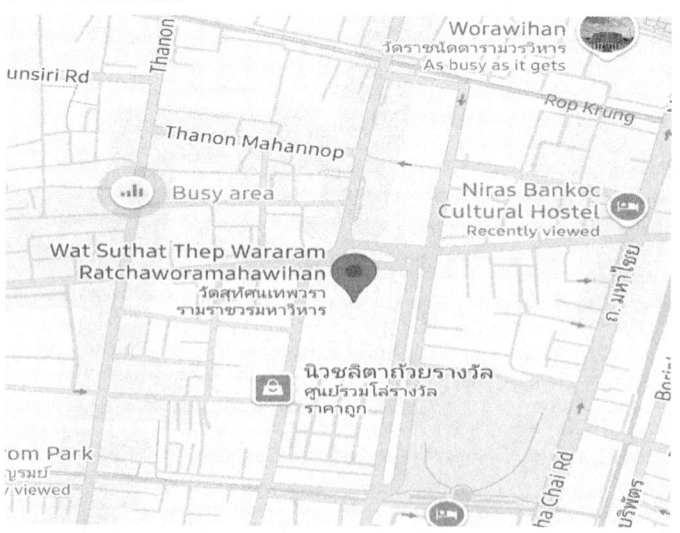

Wat Suthat, near the Giant Swing, is a tranquil retreat with an amazing, artistically decorated Buddha statue. Its tranquil courtyard and towering prominence make it an ideal site for a quiet breather while learning about the area's history.

Quiet Cafes
Bangkok's café culture has exploded in recent years, but there are still plenty of quaint, hidden corners where you can enjoy a coffee away from the masses.

The Coffee Academics
This café, located in the Thonglor district, is a heaven for coffee aficionados like myself. Its basic design and serene environment make it excellent for working or relaxing. Their distinctive brews and expertly made espresso beverages are delicious, and the atmosphere is ideal for relaxing and people-watching.

The Jam Factory
The Jam Factory, located near the Chao Phraya River, is a creative facility that functions as a café, bookstore, and art gallery. The laid-back atmosphere here is ideal for an afternoon of reading or eating light meals. I enjoy the rustic, industrial feel of the room, and the riverfront location lends a tranquil element to my stay.

Local Markets
Bangkok is well-known for its markets, but while Chatuchak and Pratunam are packed with tourists, I've discovered a few hidden treasures that I can buy like a native.

Sampeng Market
If you're willing to venture off the usual road, Sampeng Market in Chinatown is where people shop for textiles, jewelry, and everything in between. It's less polished than the major tourist markets, but that's part of its appeal. The narrow lanes are brimming with color, and I enjoy getting lost in the maze of stalls, conversing with friendly shop owners while looking for interesting items.

Or Tor Kor Market
Or Tor Kor Market, located a short walk from the more popular Chatuchak, is well-known for its fresh vegetables and genuine Thai cuisine. I frequently come here to purchase fresh herbs, fruits, and snacks that are difficult to locate in other markets. The food vendors here are wonderful, providing a

sample of local flavors in a casual, non-touristy setting.

Off-the-Beaten Path Locations
Bangkok features a few lesser-known neighborhoods that are ideal for exploring if you want to move away from the usual tourist sites.

Bang Krachao (the Green Lung of Bangkok)
Bang Krachao, located a short boat ride across the Chao Phraya River from Bangkok, is a lush, green paradise that feels worlds away from the city's sprawl. This area, known as the "Green Lung" of the city, is ideal for cycling through scenic roads, discovering local parks, and experiencing typical Thai village life. I enjoy riding a bike and riding around the serene canals, surrounded by nature.

Lumpini Park at dusk
While Lumphini Park is well-known, it's easy to overlook the peace it provides, especially in the nights when the city quiets down. I frequently go around the lake, watching the sunset over the cityscape, and occasionally I'll join a local Tai Chi

group or sit and watch the monitor lizards glide over the water.

Shopping in Bangkok

Bangkok is a shopping haven, and I can tell you from personal experience that it is one of the most fascinating cities in the world for retail therapy. Whether you're looking for expensive brands, local designer goods, or unexpected street finds, Bangkok has it all. Allow me to guide you through some of the top shopping districts that will make your trip unforgettable.

Chatuchak Market

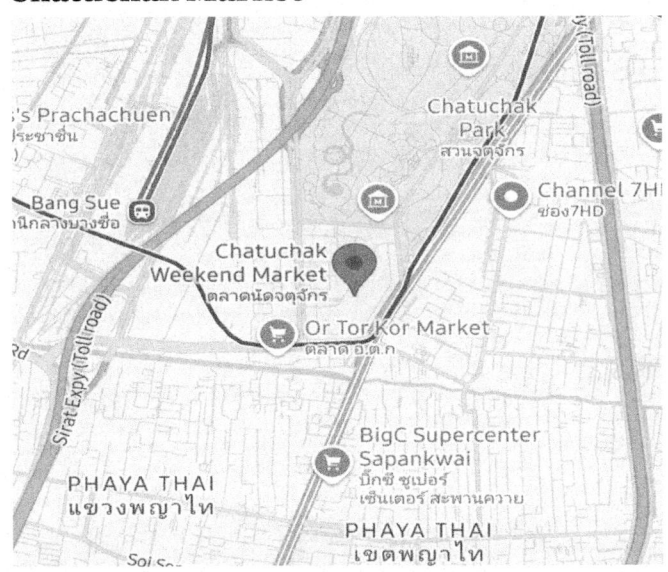

If you enjoy marketplaces, Chatuchak is a must-see destination. Also referred to as the J.J. Market is one of the world's largest outdoor markets. With over 15,000 stalls, I've spent hours getting lost here, and you're bound to find something you'll enjoy. From clothing and accessories to antiques and home décor, it's a bargain hunter's dream. The market is open on weekends, and it's better to arrive early to avoid congestion. Pro tip: Stay hydrated and wear comfy shoes, as you'll be walking for hours!

Siam Square

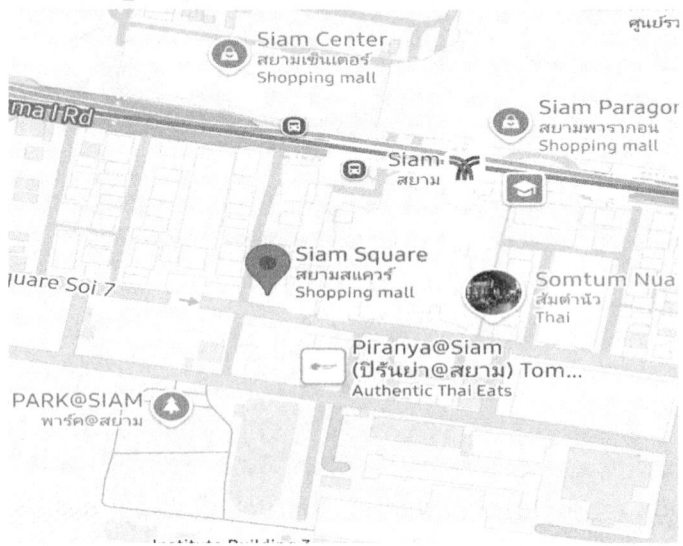

Siam Square is the core of Bangkok's popular shopping district. It's where the fashion-forward go to find the latest fashions from local designers and international brands. Personally, I enjoy the atmosphere here, which combines modern malls, street fashion, and chic boutiques. Siam Paragon is a standout, offering everything from luxury goods to exquisite cuisine. Siam Center, a more youthful shopping destination with innovative boutiques, is only a short walk away. If you want to shop and then relax with a wonderful dinner, this area features some of the best restaurants and cafes for refueling after a shopping trip.

Pratunam

When it comes to wholesale shopping, Pratunam is where I go for the best deals. Pratunam Market is well-known for its fashion, especially apparel and accessories supplied at wholesale prices. The streets are crowded with businesses selling anything from fashionable apparel to traditional Thai clothing. Don't forget to visit the Platinum apparel Mall, which is air-conditioned and has over 2,000 retailers selling affordable apparel. I've bought stylish clothes here for a fraction of the price I'd pay elsewhere in the world.

Cultural and Historical Sites

Bangkok is a city that perfectly blends the past and present, providing several opportunities to discover its rich history and vibrant culture. As soon as I stepped into the city, I was attracted by the ancient temples, beautiful palaces, and interesting museums that showcase Thailand's rich cultural history.

Museums in Bangkok

If you're anything like me and enjoy history and art, Bangkok has many fantastic museums. One of the highlights for me was the Bangkok National Museum. It is Thailand's largest museum, located near the Grand Palace, and houses a vast collection of objects highlighting the country's artistic and historical growth. From royal regalia to Buddhist art, each corner of the museum offers a tale about Thailand's history.

Another museum that I highly recommend is the Jim Thompson House. This is where I discovered the interesting story of Jim Thompson, an American businessman who helped revitalize Thailand's silk industry in the 1950s and 1960s. His traditional teak house, now a museum, showcases both Thai craftsmanship and Western influence. The museum is a tranquil sanctuary in the heart of the city, and I liked walking through the rich gardens as much as I did exploring the house.

Ancient Temples
No trip to Bangkok is complete without visiting the historic temples that are the center of the city's spiritual life. Wat Phra Kaew, often known as the Temple of the Emerald Buddha, was one of the most impressive for me. This temple, located on the grounds of the Grand Palace, is home to Thailand's most revered religious artifact, the Emerald Buddha. The delicate features of the construction, as well as the serene serenity of the surroundings, left me completely in awe. The temple's significant

connection to Thailand's royal and religious past makes it difficult not to feel reverent here.

I went to Wat Arun, the Temple of Dawn, which is one of Bangkok's most recognizable landmarks. The temple's beautiful central spire, adorned with brilliant porcelain tiles, is even more spectacular when seen from across the Chao Phraya River. It's especially beautiful at sunrise, when I went to take the perfect photograph.

For a more peaceful and less crowded experience, I recommend visiting Wat Pho, better known as the Temple of the Reclining Buddha. This temple is home to a 46-meter-long golden reclining Buddha statue. Walking around this peaceful temple complex and seeing individuals meditate deepened my admiration for Thai spiritual practices.

Cultural Experiences
While temples and museums are crucial, I also recommend seeing Bangkok's thriving cultural scene. One of my favorite experiences was going to Chinatown (Yaowarat). The small lanes are filled with gold shops, traditional Chinese medicine

kiosks, and street vendors serving delicious food. It's an ideal site to discover the cultural fusion that has shaped Bangkok's identity throughout the years. I enjoyed the sensory overload—bright colors, tantalizing fragrances, and the sounds of people going about their business.

For a more full cultural experience, attend a traditional Thai dance performance or a Muay Thai boxing event. I saw a Muay Thai match in Lumpinee Boxing Stadium, and it was one of the most exciting cultural experiences I've ever experienced. The intensity and precision of the fighters astounded me, and the atmosphere was electric.

If you're fortunate enough to visit Bangkok during one of the big festivals, such as Songkran (the Thai New Year) or Loy Krathong, you'll be able to witness the city's vibrant customs firsthand. During Songkran, the streets come alive with water battles, and it seems like the entire city is partying. It is an amazing and memorable experience!

Outdoor Activities and Parks

Bangkok is well-known for its busy streets and vibrant markets, but it also has a surprising number of green spaces and outdoor activities that provide a welcome respite from the city's hectic pace. Whether you want to explore verdant parks, go on beautiful bike excursions, or admire the beauty of the Chao Phraya River, there is something for everyone to enjoy in the outdoors.

Explore Bangkok's Parks
Lumpini Park, located in the city center, is one of the first places I recommend for a calm vacation. It is one of Bangkok's largest and most recognizable parks. As soon as I enter the park, I am met by big trees, spacious walking routes, and picturesque lakes. It's the ideal location for a morning jog or a leisurely stroll. I enjoy seeing residents practice Tai Chi by the water, as well as the occasional paddle boat drifting over the lake. It's a peaceful haven in the midst of the city's chaos.

Suan Rot Fai Park (also known as Railway Park) is another interesting park to explore. It's a great spot for cycling and picnicking, and it's close to Chatuchak Market too. The park's huge open spaces are ideal for a bike ride, and the peaceful environment makes it one of my favorite places to relax after a long day of sightseeing.

The Chao Phraya River
The Chao Phraya River offers a completely unique outdoor experience. Known as the "River of Kings," this waterway is the lifeblood of Bangkok, and touring it by boat provides a completely different perspective on the city. I enjoy hopping on a river taxi or a traditional long-tail boat to get a closer look at life along the river. Whether you're looking at temples and historical relics like Wat Arun or driving through vibrant riverbank settlements, the views from the river are spectacular. I frequently take a sunset boat to see the city's skyline light up as the sun sets over the river - it's a stunning sight that never gets old.

Bike Tours Around the City
If you're searching for a more active way to travel, I strongly recommend taking a bike trip. Cycling is one of the greatest ways to explore Bangkok up

close, particularly in places that are difficult to get by automobile. I've gone on a couple guided bike excursions, and they've always been the highlight of my travels. My favorite tour takes me through Bangkok's Old Town, where I ride past historic temples, hidden lanes, and local marketplaces. It's a fun, eco-friendly way to explore the city at a leisurely pace and find hidden gems that tourists typically overlook. Furthermore, the local guides often provide intriguing insights into Bangkok's history and culture that I would not have discovered otherwise.

For a more off-the-beaten-path bike adventure, I recommend cycling through Thonburi's canals. This path takes you to Bangkok's quieter, more traditional side, where you can observe how locals live on the lake, surrounded by beautiful foliage and wooden buildings. It's a quiet contrast to the bustling city center and allows me to see Bangkok's rich cultural legacy from a new perspective.

Chapter 4: Experiencing Bangkok's Cuisine

Introduction to Thai Cuisine

When I first had Thai cuisine, I was blown away by the brilliant colors, aromatic fragrances, and explosion of tastes that danced on my taste senses. Thai cuisine is characterized by a great balance of sweet, sour, salty, and spicy flavors, which serve as the foundation for many dishes and genuinely distinguish Thai cookery.

Key Flavours and Ingredients That Define Thai Cuisine

Sweet
Thai cuisine frequently utilizes sugar or sweeteners such as palm sugar, which provide a delicate sweetness to offset the more powerful flavors. Coconut milk, another essential ingredient, adds a creamy richness to both savory and sweet recipes.

Sour
Lime, tamarind, and vinegar are popular souring agents in Thai cuisine. The sharp tang of lime, for example, is frequently used in Thai soups such as Tom Yum, where it cuts through the heat and adds a refreshing zing.

Salty
Fish sauce (nam pla), soy sauce, and shrimp paste are the primary sources of salt in Thai cuisine. Fish sauce is a Thai culinary staple that adds a rich

umami taste to a variety of foods, including curries and stir fries.

Spicy

Thai cuisine is known for its spiciness, which is derived from fresh chilies and chili pastes. Bird's eye chilies are small but spicy, and they can be found in a variety of recipes, including Pad Thai and Green Curry. The heat is frequently adjusted with the other flavors to create a harmonious experience, so it does not overpower the palate but instead provides a lingering warmth.

Herbs and Aromatics

Thai cuisine likewise relies extensively on aromatic herbs. Lemongrass, galangal, kaffir lime leaves, and Thai basil give meals a fragrant and rich flavor. These ingredients are frequently used in broths, soups, and curries, giving Thai cuisine its distinct fresh, herbal flavor.

Curry Pastes

Thai curries are flavorful and diverse, with red, green, and yellow curry pastes at the heart of many dishes. These pastes are created by crushing fresh herbs, spices, and chilies into a paste that is then used as the foundation for stews, soups, and stir-fries. Each paste has its own distinct flavor profile, with green curry being the most spicy and yellow curry being the gentler and somewhat sweeter alternative.

Street Food

Bangkok's street food culture is one of the city's most interesting and savory attractions. As soon as you enter the bustling streets, you'll see sellers lining the roads, sizzling woks, and the alluring perfume of spices floating through the air. It's not just food; it's a lifestyle. Whether you're a seasoned eater or new to the world of street cuisine, Bangkok has something for everyone.

Must-Try Dishes

Pad Thai
Pad Thai is an absolute must-try for anybody visiting Bangkok. This stir-fried noodle dish, composed with rice noodles, shrimp or chicken, peanuts, bean sprouts, and a tangy tamarind sauce,

is both filling and delicious. For the greatest Pad Thai, go to Thip Samai near the ancient city (Samran Rat). The crowds here attest to its genuineness, and the dish is served with a substantial portion of fresh lime and chili on the side, allowing you to tailor the flavor to your preferences.

Som Tum (green papaya salad)
Som Tum, a spicy green papaya salad with chilies, lime, fish sauce, and palm sugar topped with crushed peanuts, is a delicious but scorching food. You can find it at street stalls all around Bangkok, but for a remarkable experience, go to Soi Convent, where the merchants specialize in fresh, tangy versions of this traditional delicacy.

Mango Sticky Rice (Khao Niew Mamuang)
If you're yearning for something sweet, Mango Sticky Rice is a must-have. The mix of ripe, juicy mango with sweet, sticky coconut rice is simply divine. One of the greatest places to try it is on Sampeng Lane in Chinatown, where the merchants provide the ideal blend of sweetness and texture.

Satay (grilled skewers)
These soft grilled skewers of chicken, pork, or beef are marinated in a fragrant spice blend and topped with a creamy peanut sauce. Satay stalls may be found all across the city, but Sukhumvit Soi 38 is particularly well-known for its late-night offerings.

Khao man gai (chicken rice)
This simple yet comforting recipe features poached chicken, fragrant rice cooked in chicken broth, and a tasty dipping sauce. It's a famous comfort dish, and Khao Man Gai Pratunam is one of the most well-known places to get some.

Boat Noodle (Kuay Teow Reua)
Boat noodles, a popular local dish, are rich and delicious, served in small bowls with pork or beef. The broth is flavorful, and the dish is generally garnished with herbs, chiles, and a touch of lime. For an authentic experience, visit Victory Monument, where boat noodle vendors line the streets.

Where to Find the Best Street Food?

Bangkok is separated into neighborhoods, each with its own specialties, so make sure to explore the city to get the greatest street food.

Chinatown (Yaowarat)

This region is a foodie's dream, particularly at night. From dim sum to roasted duck, you'll discover some of the best Chinese-influenced street food here. Don't miss the Yaowarat Night Market for a gourmet treat.

Sukhumvit Soi 38

This area is a must-visit for night owls, with booths selling everything from satay to mango sticky rice. It's an excellent area to try late-night street cuisine and mix with both residents and tourists.

Chatuchak Market

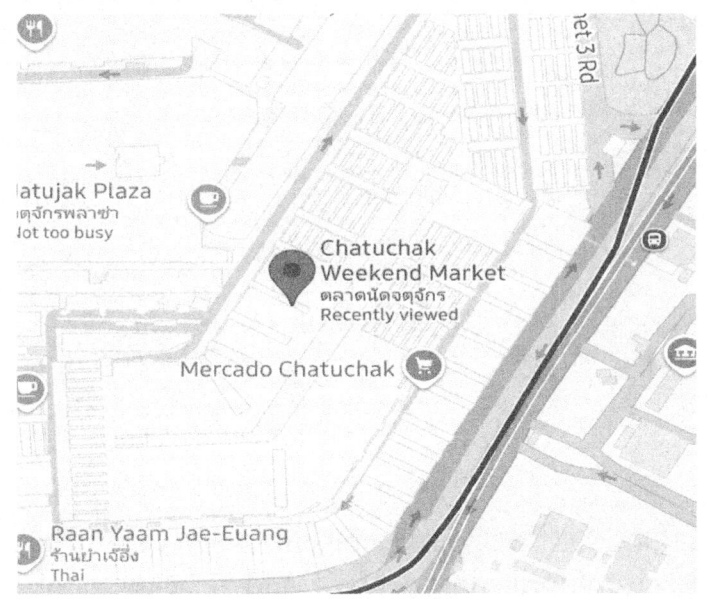

Chatuchak is well-known for its shopping, but it is also a popular street food destination. From classic Thai cuisine to lesser-known regional specialties, you'll be able to experience a wide range of local treats here. Be sure to try the grilled pork skewers or the spicy boat noodles.

Pratunam Market

This area is recognized not only for its shopping, but also for its inexpensive and delicious street cuisine. Stalls sell fried noodles, grilled meats, and sweet pastries.

Khaosan Road

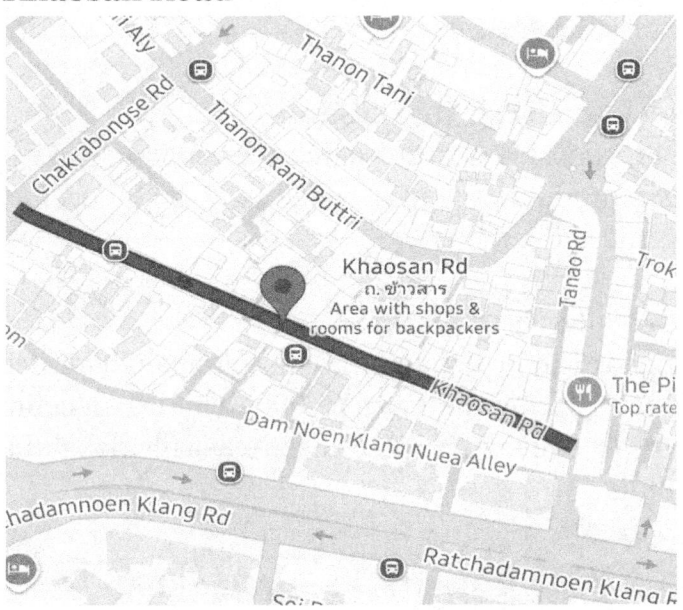

Despite its popularity as a tourist destination, Khao San Road continues to offer a variety of street food options. Try the pad see ew (stir-fried noodles) or a tasty coconut ice cream.

A Few Tips to enjoy Street food in Bangkok

Follow the Natives

If a stall is packed with locals, it's usually a good hint that the food is worth trying. Locals know the greatest places!

Check for fresh Ingredients
When choosing a stall, search for vendors who use fresh produce, as this suggests a high level of hygiene and quality.

Drink plenty of water!
Bangkok can be hot and humid, so remain hydrated when exploring the city's culinary culture. Coconut water or chilled Thai iced tea are usually delightful options.

Best Restaurants in Bangkok

As a foodie, one of the first things I do when I arrive in a new city is explore the local cuisine. Bangkok's mix of street food vendors and world-class gourmet dining did not disappoint. Whether you want the simplicity of a hot bowl of noodles or a lavish Michelin-star experience, the city has it all. Here's my pick of the greatest places to dine in Bangkok, from basic street food vendors to exquisite, high-end restaurants.

Street Food Gems
Let's start with the heart and spirit of Bangkok's cuisine culture: street food. This is where you'll discover the most authentic and tasty meals, typically prepared right in front of you.

Yaowarat (Chinatown)

No vacation to Bangkok is complete without a stop in Chinatown. The colorful streets are lined with food stalls selling delicious meals including Dim Sum, Mango Sticky Rice, and Khao Moo Daeng (roast pork rice). I appreciate grabbing a fast bite from one of the seafood carts, where you can get fresh prawns or crab, which are often barbecued right on the spot.

Soi 38 Sukhumvit

Another place I can't get enough of is Soi 38 in Sukhumvit, where street food vendors provide a range of traditional Thai meals. My favorite dish here is Pad Thai from the corner stall, where the noodles are crunchy and full of flavor.

Rahan Jay Fai

For something more iconic (and Michelin-starred), visit Raan Jay Fai. Jay Fai is a street food icon in Bangkok, well known for her crab omelette and drunken noodles. It's street food elevated to the level of art.

Mid-range Dining

If you want to have a more refined experience without breaking the bank, Bangkok has a selection of restaurants that serve superb meals in a more relaxed atmosphere.

Thip Samai

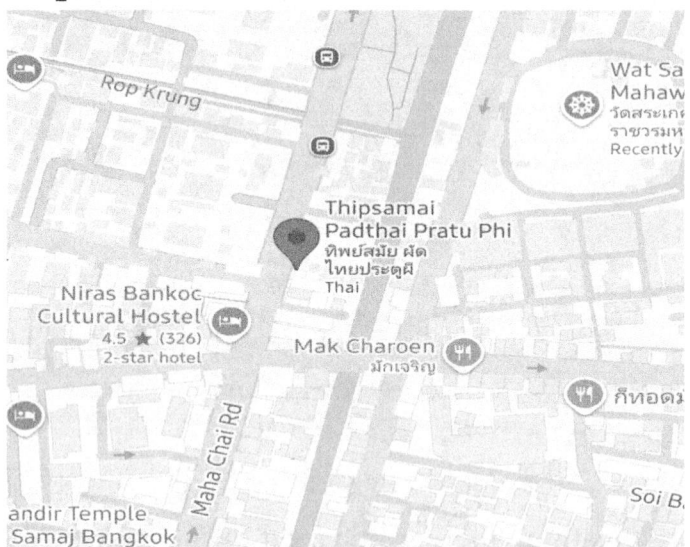

Thip Samai is well-known as one of the greatest spots for Pad Thai, thanks to its fresh ingredients and characteristic preparation method, which involves wrapping egg around the noodles. It's inexpensive and always packed with locals, which is fantastic news for any foodie.

Soul Food Mahanakorn

This restaurant is one of my favorites for genuine Thai cuisine with a modern twist. The Khao Soi (a northern Thai curry noodle meal) here is delicious, and the atmosphere is warm and welcoming. Their cocktails are definitely worth trying, making it an excellent choice for lunch and evening.

Cabbages and Condoms

If you're searching for a unique eating experience, Cabbages & Condoms serves exquisite Thai cuisine in a socially conscious environment. This restaurant supports family planning activities, and the quirky décor (including condoms!) creates a lively atmosphere. The Massaman Curry and Tom Yum Goong are also excellent choices here.

Fine Dining

For special events or simply to pamper yourself, Bangkok's fine dining scene is a game changer. Here are my top recommendations for unforgettable meals:

Gaa

Gaa combines traditional Indian cuisines with Thai elements. The food is meticulously prepared and elegantly presented. It's a dining experience that seems like a journey, and the tasting menu is highly recommended. The tastes are robust yet balanced, and the creative take on Indian food makes this one of my favorite fine-dining establishments.

Sirocco
Sirocco at the Lebua State Tower is the place to go for a breathtaking view and excellent cuisine. The rooftop setting provides stunning views of the metropolitan skyline, and the Mediterranean-inspired menu never disappoints. A drink of champagne while viewing the sunset is something I always look forward to.

Nahm
I can't discuss great eating in Bangkok without mentioning Nahm. It's one of the world's top Thai restaurants, with a Michelin star for its expertly executed, enhanced classic dishes. Som Tum (Papaya Salad) and Green Curry are must-haves here, prepared with outstanding skill and love.

Night Markets and Food Festivals

The best way to experience Bangkok's lively street food culture is to visit the city's famed night markets and food festivals. As a foodie, I can assure you that these markets are a must-see, delivering not only delectable local fare but also a true experience of the city's culture. Let me walk you through some of my favorite sites, and I'll even give you some recommendations on things you should certainly try!

The Iconic Chatuchak Night Market
While Chatuchak Market is well-known as a daytime shopping destination, its night market provides an equally fascinating experience. I truly love coming here once the sun has set. It's much colder, and the crowds tend to clear out, making it ideal for a relaxing stroll. You'll discover a wide variety of street food shops selling everything from Pad Thai to mango sticky rice. For a truly Bangkok experience, don't miss the grilled chicken skewers or the som tam (spicy green papaya salad), which are packed with robust, fresh tastes that are difficult to surpass.

Ratchada Train Night Market

Another favorite of mine is the Ratchada Train Night Market, also known as Talad Rot Fai. This market blends the appeal of vintage goods with a large number of food stands. The mood is upbeat, and the market truly comes alive in the evening. I enjoy grabbing a cool Thai iced drink and strolling around trying everything I can get my hands on. The fried chicken wings and banana roti are standouts, but don't overlook the grilled seafood, which is both fresh and tasty. The open-air atmosphere makes it ideal for a night out with friends or family.

Asiatique The Riverfront

Asiatique the Riverfront is a terrific place to spend a relaxing evening. This market, located along the Chao Phraya River, offers shopping, entertainment, and food in one location. It's the perfect venue if you want a more relaxed atmosphere with stunning views of the river at night. The food here is superb, including a variety of Thai staples such as tom yum goong (spicy shrimp soup) and pad see ew (stir-fried noodles). Asiatique also hosts various cuisine events throughout the year, so if you're lucky enough to visit during one, you'll have the opportunity to experience even more local delicacies.

Bangkok Street Food Festivals
If you visit Bangkok during one of its many food festivals, you're in for a treat. I enjoy how these festivals bring together the best street food sellers, chefs, and local artists. Events like the Bangkok Street Food Festival highlight the city's culinary diversity and provide an excellent opportunity to experience different cuisine all in one location. The festivals typically include live cooking demos, food stalls, and contests in which sellers compete for the title of "Best Street Food." There is also a sense of community among foodies, and the atmosphere is electrifying. It's one of the most enjoyable ways to immerse yourself in the city's culinary scene.

Tips for Exploring Bangkok's Night Markets and Food Festivals

Go Hungry!

The variety of food at these markets is tremendous, so prepare to taste as many things as possible. You may always share with friends and try a little bit of everything!

Cash is King
Most food stalls only accept cash, so make sure you have lots of Thai baht. Some marketplaces may offer ATMs, however it is always advisable to be prepared.

Be Adventurous
Don't hesitate to try anything new. From fried insects to unusual fruits, Bangkok's night markets provide a world of tastes that you may not discover elsewhere.

Stay Hydrated
The heat and spice can get to you, so stay hydrated or try a refreshing coconut water to cool down.

Traditional Thai Dining Etiquette

When dining in Thailand, there are a few traditional customs and practices that will not only enhance your meal but also help you blend in with the locals. As a first-time traveler, I discovered that respecting these dining etiquette guidelines made my experience more real and considerate. Here is what I've learned about eating like a local in Thailand.

Family-style Dining
In Thailand, meals are often served family-style, with various dishes put in the center of the table for everyone to share. This communal approach promotes camaraderie, and it's crucial to remember that no meal is intended for a single person. If you're dining with locals, don't be shy—share the variety of foods and try everything.

Use of Utensils
Thailand's primary utensils are a spoon and a fork. However, the spoon is used for eating, but the fork is only used to press food onto the spoon. It is normal to hold the spoon with your right hand and the fork with your left. Chopsticks are generally

used to eat noodle dishes like pad Thai or boat noodles, although for most meals, a spoon and fork will do.

Do not Stick your fork in your Mouth
When using a fork, remember that it is not intended to go immediately into your mouth. It is solely utilized to transfer food to your spoon, which is subsequently delivered to your mouth. It is considered disrespectful to eat directly with a fork.

Serve yourself Moderately
While it is tempting to fill your plate with all of the delectable food available, it is considered polite in Thailand to serve yourself a little portion at first. Going back for more is totally acceptable, but taking too much at first can be perceived as greedy. This also enables everyone at the table to share without running out of dishes.

Wait for the Elders
Respect for seniors is particularly essential in Thai society, even meals. If you're dining with natives, wait until the oldest person at the table starts eating before you dig in. This demonstrates respect and

highlights the significance of hierarchy in Thai culture.

Do not Rush your Meal
Meals in Thailand are designed to be taken slowly and with excellent company. Dining is more than just eating; it's a chance to unwind and connect. Do not rush through your lunch; instead, take your time savoring the tastes and enjoying the conversation. In fact, Thai lunches can go for hours, especially when you're sharing stories with friends and family.

Express Gratitude
After finishing your dinner, it is traditional to express thankfulness. Saying "khop khun krap/ka" (thank you) is an appropriate way to express gratitude for the food. It's a small gesture that goes a long way toward reflecting Thai kindness.

The Bill
If you are dining in a group, it is customary for the person who invited the others to cover the bill. However, in more modern circumstances, dividing the bill has become more prevalent. It is courteous

to silently accept the bill rather than dispute about who will pay.

Sharing is Key
Sharing food is fundamental to Thai cuisine, and it is frequently more important than completing everything on your plate. It's nice to leave a little food behind to indicate that you've had enough, but if someone gives you more, don't be hesitant to accept it!

Do not Tip Excessively
While tipping is not required in Thailand, it is appreciated for excellent service, particularly in more expensive places. A gratuity of roughly 10% is appropriate if you believe the service was exceptional. However, bear in mind that tipping excessively can make the natives uncomfortable, so keep it modest.

Chapter 5: Bangkok's Vibrant Nightlife

Rooftop Bars and Nightclubs

When the sun goes down in Bangkok, the city changes into a glittering spectacle of lights, music, and lively energy. Bangkok's nightlife provides something for everyone, from sipping cocktails high above the cityscape to dancing the night away. I've visited some of the city's most magnificent rooftop bars and bustling nightclubs, and these are the places you shouldn't miss.

Rooftop Bars offer Cocktails with a view

Sky Bar in Lebua State Tower

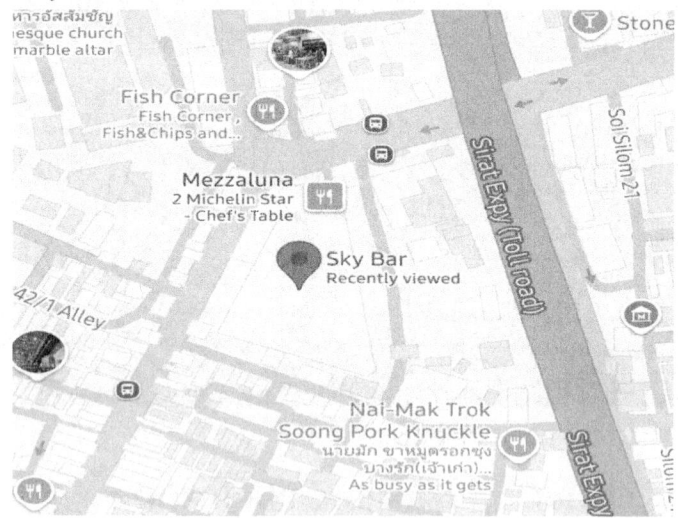

If you've seen The Hangover Part II, you're already familiar with Sky Bar, which is one of the world's most recognizable rooftop bars. Sky Bar, located on the 63rd floor of the Lebua State Tower, offers breathtaking views of the city and the Chao Phraya River. Watching the sunset with a martini in hand seems magical. The drinks are high-end (and expensive), but the experience is well worth it. Try the Hangovertini, their signature cocktail, as a lighthearted tribute to their Hollywood renown.

Vertigo and Moon Bar, Banyan Tree Bangkok

Another must-see rooftop attraction is Moon Bar, which is located on the 61st level of the Banyan Tree Hotel. The open-air architecture makes you feel as if you are floating in the sky, with the lights of Bangkok stretching eternally below you. I propose the Vertigo Sunset, which is a delightful combination of pineapple, cranberry, and lime juice with a dash of Malibu. Pair it with their light bites, such as grilled seafood, for an unforgettable evening.

Octave Rooftop Lounge and Bar

For a more relaxing and less touristy atmosphere, visit Octave, located on the 45th level of the Marriott Hotel Sukhumvit. Octave, unlike some other rooftop bars, has a modern, fashionable, and welcoming atmosphere, making it ideal for a younger population. What I like best about this place is the multi-level design—you can switch between floors for different atmospheres. One of my favorite drinks here is the Thai Mojito with lemongrass and ginger!

Tichuca Rooftop Bar

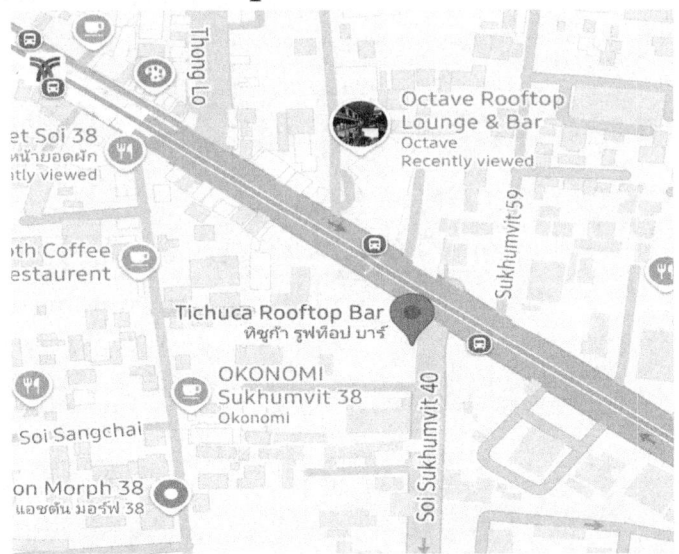

Tijuca is a relatively new addition to Bangkok's rooftop scene, but it has rapidly become a local favorite. It's a jungle-themed bar on the 46th floor, famed for its eye-catching neon "tree" display. At night, the tree illuminates, providing a wonderful, otherworldly atmosphere. Their tropical cocktails are wonderful, and the rates are lower than other rooftop bars.

Bangkok Nightclubs

Route 66 Club

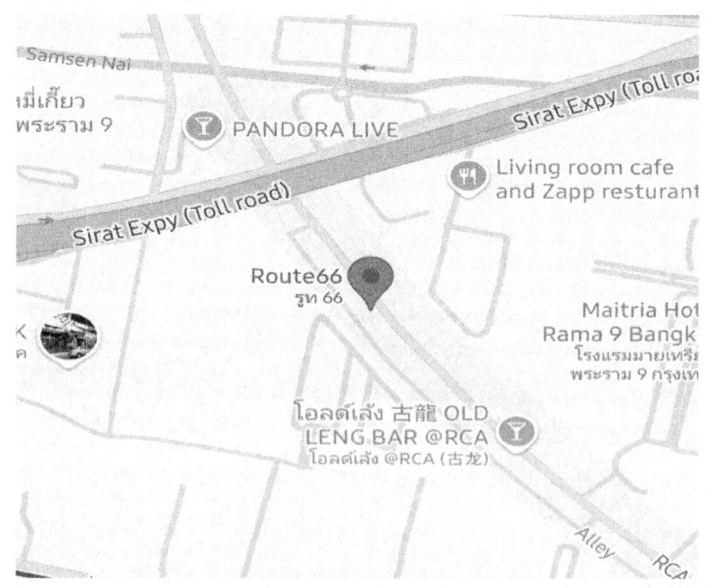

If you want to party all night, head to Route 66 on Royal City Avenue (RCA). This club is a major nighttime attraction with multiple zones featuring everything from EDM and hip-hop to live bands. It's always full of energy, and both residents and tourists like it. The drinks are decently priced, and what about the music? Completely electric.

BEAM

For a sophisticated, high-tech clubbing experience, I recommend BEAM in Thonglor. The sound system here is next-level, with deep, thundering sounds that will make your heart race. BEAM attracts Bangkok's stylish population, and the music focuses on underground techno, house, and hip-hop. Pro tip: Arrive early as it tends to fill up quickly!

Sing Sing Theatre

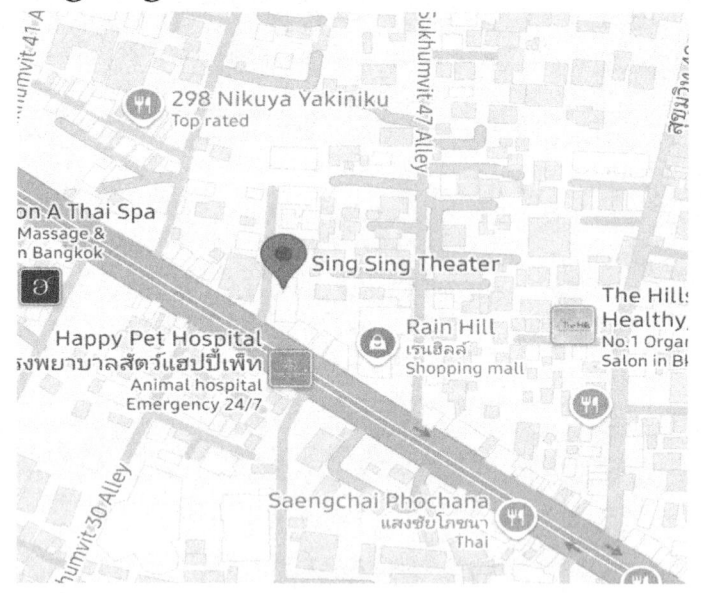

This nightclub in Sukhumvit is a work of art—truly, one of the most gorgeously constructed clubs I've ever seen. Sing Sing Theater combines a modern aesthetic with traditional Asian-inspired decor, resulting in an almost mystical ambiance. The DJs here spin a diverse mix of EDM, house, and pop, and the crowd is always upbeat.

Levels Club and Lounge

Levels, located on Sukhumvit Soi 11, offers a mix of top 40 music, EDM, and live acts. The club includes several locations, including an outdoor patio for when you need a break from the dancing floor. It's popular among visitors and expats, so there's always someone to party with.

Cultural Nightlife

When the sun goes down in Bangkok, the city transforms into a lively mix of traditional and modern entertainment. For those wishing to immerse themselves in Thai culture after dark, Bangkok has a unique selection of cultural nightlife alternatives that combine the ancient and the new.

One of my particular faves is to see traditional Thai dance performances. These magnificent dances are frequently performed in cultural institutions, hotels, and restaurants, including the Siam Niramit Theatre, which is one of the world's largest stage shows. Watching the elegant motions of the dancers in their bright, complex costumes deepens my love for Thai history and mythology. The performances depict stories about the country's rich cultural legacy, frequently incorporating themes of love, religion, and nature. It's an experience that never ceases to amaze me.

Another cultural highlight that should not be missed is Muay Thai, Thailand's traditional martial art. It's more than just a sport; it's an integral element of Thai culture. I highly recommend watching a Muay Thai bout at either the old Rajadamnern Stadium or the Lumpinee Boxing Stadium. These venues showcase some of the most thrilling and authentic fights in the nation. The atmosphere is electrifying, and the fighters' intensity, along with the rituals and music, creates a memorable experience. I've never left a fight without feeling thoroughly engulfed in the sport's excitement and its place in Thai culture.

Bangkok has a plethora of live music venues that offer a superb blend of classic and contemporary sounds. From jazz clubs on Sukhumvit to local live bands like Saxophone Pub near Victory Monument, there's always somewhere to listen to fantastic music. If I'm looking for something truly Thai, I'll go to a Siam Square location where traditional Thai instruments are frequently used in live performances, merging with current tunes to produce a particularly Bangkokian sound.

Bangkok's Entertainment Districts

Bangkok is a city that never sleeps, and its entertainment districts contribute significantly to its vibrancy and excitement. Whether you're seeking world-class nightlife, fashionable bars, cultural events, or even the city's famed red-light districts, there's something for everyone. Allow me to walk you through some of the most notable sites I've had the opportunity to visit.

Sukhumvit

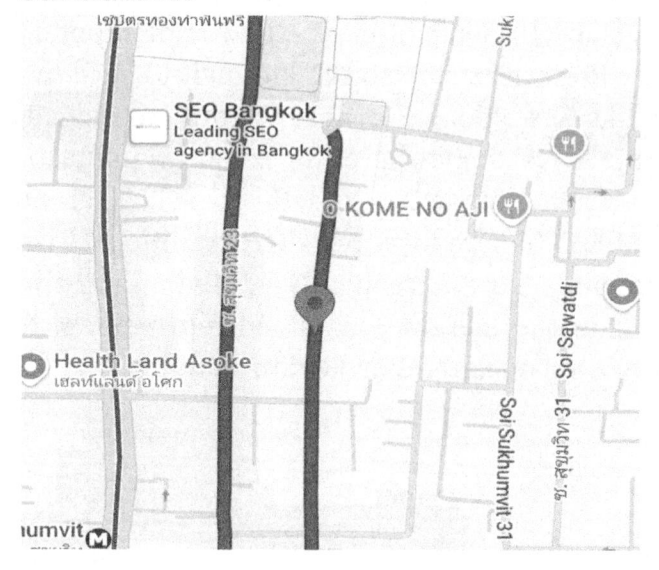

Sukhumvit is one of Bangkok's most vibrant and cosmopolitan neighborhoods, with a mix of expensive hotels, international restaurants, fashionable bars, and an ever-changing nightlife scene. As I walk down Sukhumvit Road, I can't help but notice the sophisticated malls, like Terminal 21 and EmQuartier, where I can shop for both luxury and unique, odd stuff. But the real pleasure begins when I enter the narrow sois (side streets), which are where the local nightlife thrives. Bars, nightclubs, and rooftop lounges, such as Octave, offer breathtaking views of the city, making them ideal for an evening out. The region also includes Soi Cowboy, one of the city's most well-known red-light districts, where neon lights gleam and the nightlife is vibrant. It has a reputation, but it also draws curious foreigners seeking to experience the raw energy of Bangkok's entertainment scene.

Silom

Silom is another region that provides a more diverse range of entertainment. It's regarded as a business hub during the day, but as the sun goes down, it transforms into a thriving nightlife destination. The streets are lined with everything from laid-back cafes to rooftop bars that offer panoramic views of the city skyline. Patpong, Bangkok's oldest red-light district, stands out to me. While its notoriety is mostly based on the adult entertainment business, Patpong also has a thriving night market where I can bargain for everything from souvenirs to apparel. I frequently stop by to pick up some local souvenirs before heading to a quieter bar in the neighborhood. For a more refined experience, I recommend visiting the Sky Bar at the Lebua Hotel, which was made famous by the film The Hangover Part II. The view of the city from the 63rd floor is simply breathtaking.

Khaosan Road

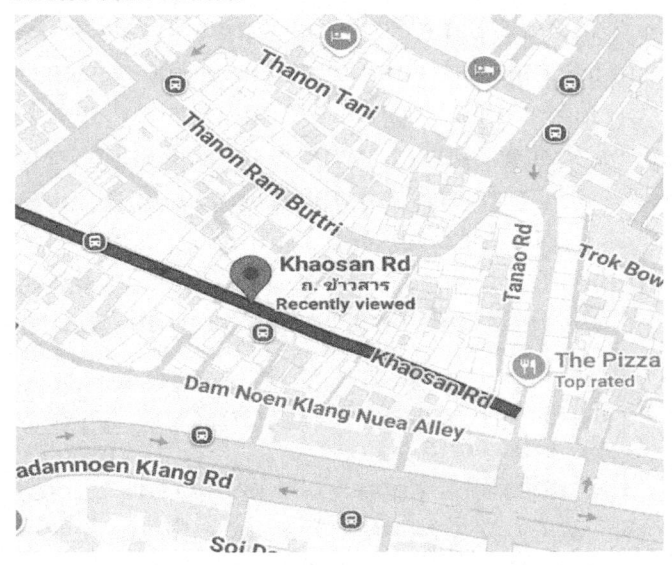

Khao San Road is a backpacker's paradise, and I must admit that it's one of my favorite places to unwind after a long day of sightseeing. This chaotic, colorful street is lined with lively bars, street food vendors, and shops selling everything from fake IDs to inexpensive clothing. There's something uniquely charming about the vibe here, with tourists and locals mingling, laughing, and enjoying the atmosphere. The drinks are inexpensive, the food is delicious, and the party atmosphere is nonstop. Khao San Road isn't just about partying; it also serves some of Bangkok's most memorable street food, including pad Thai and mango sticky rice. If you prefer something more quiet, the nearby Sampeng Lane Market, with its local shops and street stalls, provides an intriguing glimpse into Bangkok's old-world charm. Still, Khao San is best known for its low-cost party scene, which is a great place to unwind and meet people from all over the world.

Red Light Districts
While the more well-known red-light districts, such as Soi Cowboy and Nana Plaza, have their place in Bangkok's nightlife, it is important to note that they

do not represent the entirety of the city's entertainment offerings. These areas are well-known for their adult-themed shows and nightlife, and while some may find them shocking, they are part of the city's diverse culture. It's a good idea to go with an open mind, respect the workers and their craft, and be aware of potential scams. These areas can be enjoyable to explore, but I recommend remaining vigilant and taking precautions to ensure your safety.

Night Markets and Evening Experiences

One of my favorite ways to experience Bangkok's vibrant energy after sunset is by visiting its famous night markets. Bangkok truly comes alive at night, and these markets are a mix of shopping, eating, and soaking in the local atmosphere. Whether you're a foodie, a shopper, or just looking for a fun place to explore, there's a night market for everyone.

Asiatique The Riverfront

Asiatique is one of those places where modern meets traditional, and trust me, it's perfect for an evening stroll. Located near the Chao Phraya River, this market feels like a blend of a night bazaar and an open-air mall. What I enjoy most about Asiatique is its stunning riverbank views—imagine wandering down the river while shopping through over 1,500 shops and 40 restaurants. It's a terrific area for both shopping and dining.

The ambiance here is easygoing yet energetic, and the market is beautifully lit up at night. You'll discover everything from handmade crafts and clothes to souvenirs and accessories. Don't forget to ride the Asiatique Sky, a gigantic Ferris wheel that provides you amazing views of Bangkok's cityscape at night—definitely one for the memory books.

Pro tip: Asiatique gets packed after 7 PM, so arriving a little earlier (about 5 PM) lets you appreciate the venue without feeling rushed. Plus, you may grab some street cuisine while you wait for the sunset.

Talad Rot Fai (Train Market)

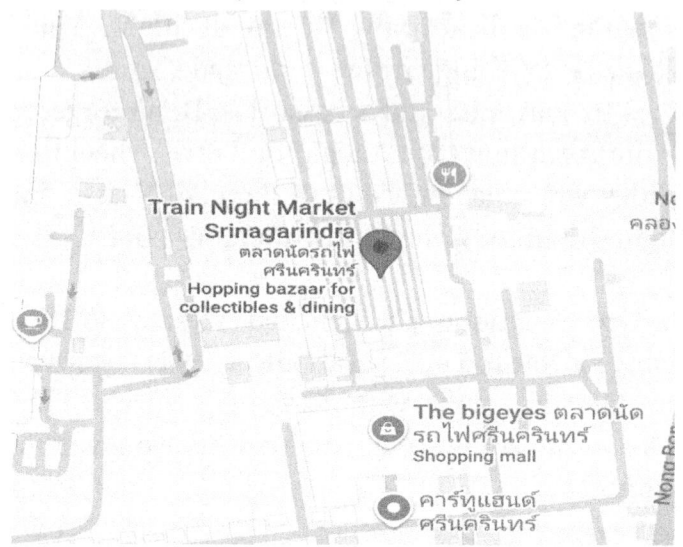

If you're wanting a more real and retro shopping experience, Talad Rot Fai—often nicknamed the Train Night Market—is where you should go. I adore how this market combines together an antique atmosphere, unique treasures, and wonderful food in one huge outdoor location.

The market is split into parts, so it's easy to get lost in the enjoyment. You'll come upon vintage stuff like ancient cameras, retro signage, and unique antiques in one section, and in another, trendy clothing, handcrafted crafts, and accessories. It's like walking inside a time capsule with a modern touch!

And let's talk about the food—seriously, come hungry. From grilled seafood and skewers to Thai desserts and cool coconut ice cream, you'll want to sample everything. For a real local delicacy, try moo ping (grilled pork skewers) with a refreshing cha yen (Thai iced tea).

What is the best part? The prices are reasonable, and bargaining is part of the enjoyment. Simply be courteous and kind, and you may walk away with a terrific offer.

Why do these Markets Stand Out?
Visiting Bangkok's night markets is more than just shopping; it is an experience. You are surrounded by lights, music, laughing, and the perfume of food, which draws you in at every turn. Whether you're taking in the riverside charm of Asiatique or embracing the eclectic energy of Talad Rot Fai, these markets encapsulate the essence of Bangkok's nightlife.

Relaxing and Unwinding

After a day of visiting Bangkok's busy streets, I want a gentler side of the city—one where I could slow down, unwind, and enjoy the calmer moments. Fortunately, Bangkok has a plethora of serene getaways, from world-class spas to soothing wellness facilities to lesser-known peaceful locales hidden away from the frenzy.

Exploring Bangkok's Spas

Bangkok's spa culture is world-renowned, and after experiencing a few personally, I can assure you that it is not to be missed. Whether you choose a lavish treatment in a five-star hotel or a traditional Thai massage in a friendly local environment, there is something for everyone.

Oasis Spa (Sukhumvit)

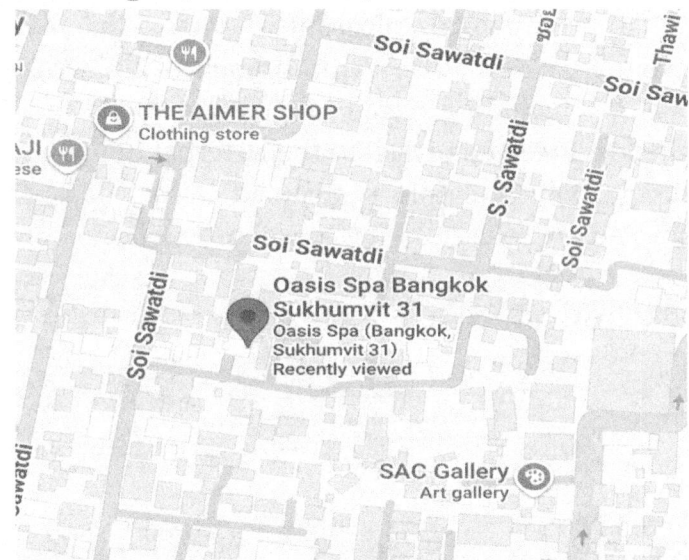

Hidden in the heart of Sukhumvit, Oasis Spa stands up to its name. Walking in is like entering another world: a verdant garden paradise with relaxing music and the aroma of lemongrass in the air. I chose their Traditional Thai Massage, which helped me relax after hours of walking. Their therapists are extremely excellent, and I left feeling like a completely different person.

Let's Relax Spa

Let's Relax Spa is ideal if you're short on time yet want a professional, pleasant service. This is a convenient alternative, with branches all across Bangkok, including retail areas like Siam and Thonglor. I treated myself to their Herbal Compress Massage, which employs steamed herbal bags to relieve aching muscles—it was well worth it.

The Peninsula Spa

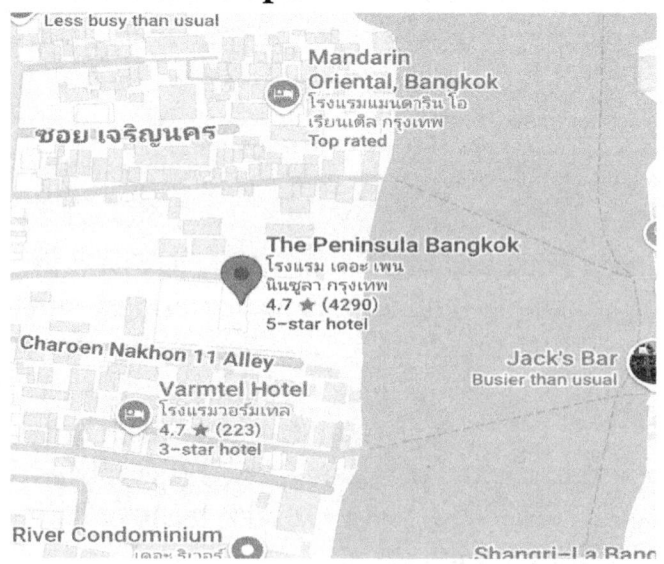

For sheer luxury, The Peninsula Spa stands out. The tranquil riverfront vistas enhance the overall experience. I scheduled an Ayurvedic Oil Massage, and it felt like an escape into ecstasy. If you're celebrating a special occasion or simply want to indulge, this is the place.

Wellness Centers
Relaxation can be more than just getting a massage; it can also mean reconnecting with your mind and body. I visited a few wellness centers in Bangkok, and they did not disappoint.

Yogatique Bangkok

Yogatique, located in a quiet part of Sukhumvit, is a hidden gem for yoga enthusiasts. They offer Hatha and Vinyasa yoga lessons for beginners as well as advanced workshops. I took their Sunset Flow session, and the relaxation I felt afterwards was precisely what I needed.

Rasayana Retreat

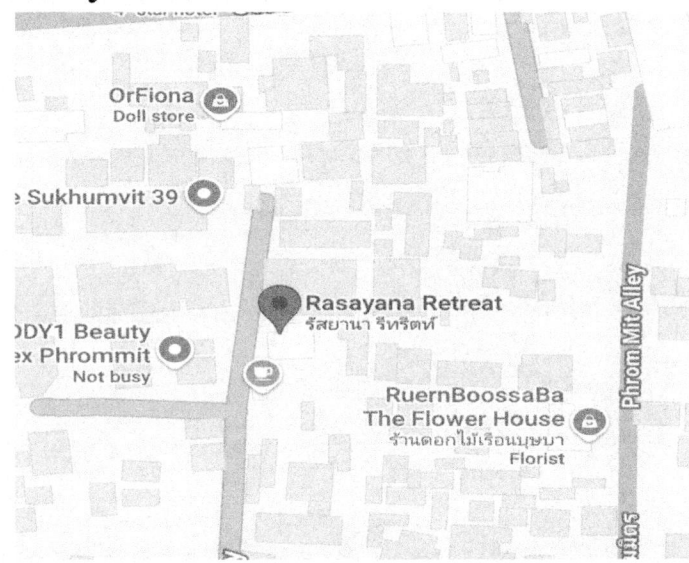

Rasayana Retreat, located in the beautiful Phrom Phong district, specializes in holistic health. They provide detox programs, organic juices, and vegan meals, which I sampled during a meditation session. Their smoothies are delicious, particularly the Cacao Bliss. It's a haven for everyone wishing to recharge their body and mind.

Quiet Escapes

In the midst of Bangkok's vibrant hum, I discovered several peaceful locations where I could simply rest, sit, and breathe.

Benjakitti Park

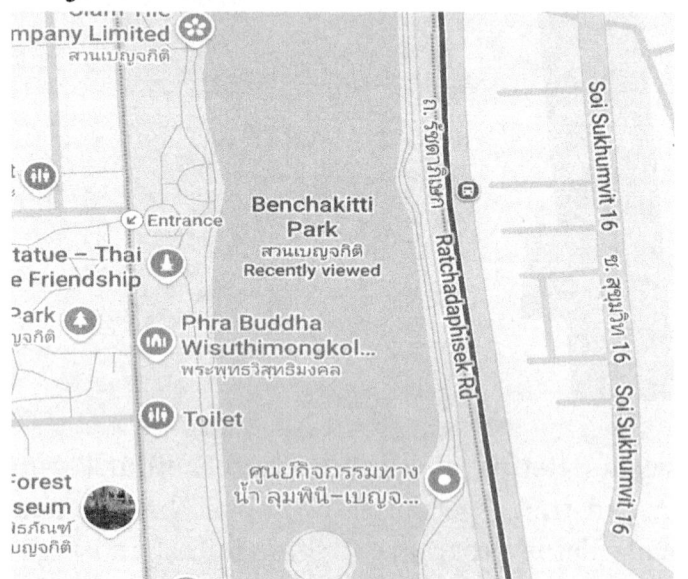

Benjakitti Park, a tranquil getaway right in the city heart, is one of my favorite places to relax. I went in the late afternoon, and the views of the lake, surrounded by greenery and the Bangkok cityscape, were breathtaking. Renting a bike or walking down the route after sunset is a relaxing experience that I highly recommend.

Wat Prayoon

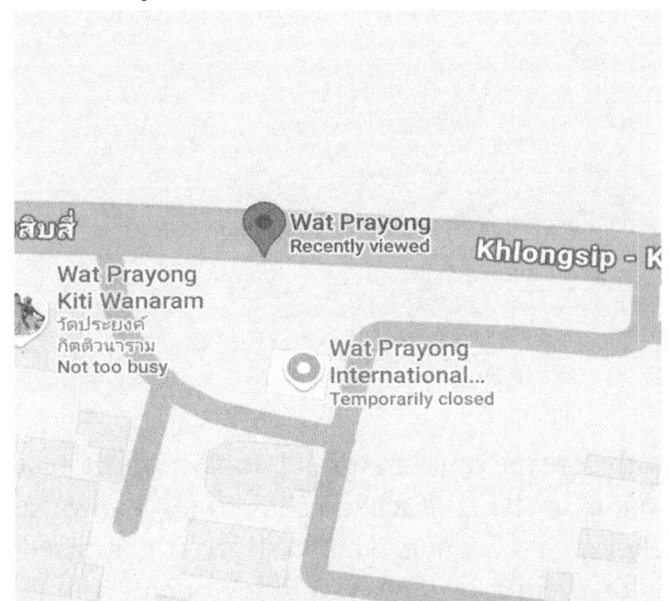

While many temples in Bangkok are overcrowded, Wat Prayoon is surprisingly peaceful. It's a quiet spot for reflection on the city's Thonburi side. I spent an hour examining the white chedi and feeding the turtles in the pond—small pleasures that made my stay memorable.

Bang Kachao

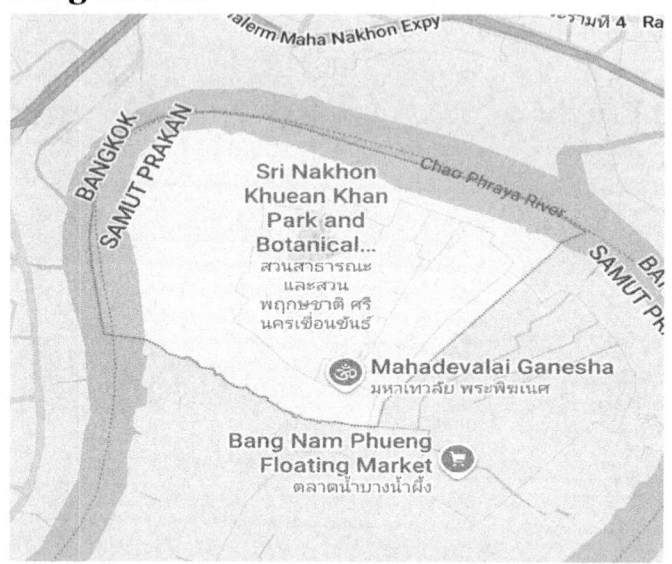

To truly escape into nature, I took a short boat excursion to Bang Kachao, sometimes known as Bangkok's Green Lung. This vast green paradise is ideal for cycling or simply walking about. The air feels cleaner here, and you might easily forget you're so near to the city.

Chapter 6: Shopping in Bangkok

Markets to Visit

Bangkok is a city where shopping is more than a pleasure; it is an experience. The city has a variety of marketplaces to suit every taste, from enormous shops full of trinkets to quiet floating markets where you can buy fresh food directly off a boat. I've been to many of these marketplaces and can't wait to share the highlights with you.

Chatuchak Weekend Market

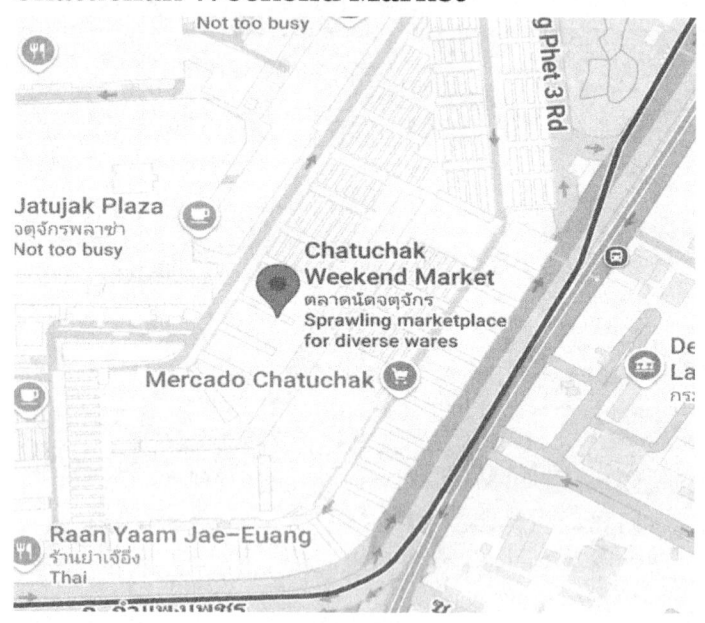

Chatuchak, or JJ Market as the locals know it, is a must-see for anybody visiting Bangkok. This gigantic weekend market is one of the world's largest, with over 15,000 vendors. It's more than simply a market—it's an adventure! I could easily spend hours exploring its maze of lanes. The market is divided into parts, with each selling something unique.

What To Buy

Clothing
Chatuchak is a fashionista's dream, with everything from contemporary streetwear to boho-chic pieces. The pricing is reasonable, and the designs are one-of-a-kind and difficult to locate elsewhere.

Home Decor
Are you looking for eccentric, handcrafted goods for your home? You'll discover everything from vintage furniture to locally crafted artwork.

Antiques and Collectibles
If you enjoy collecting, the antique section has old coins, traditional Thai goods, and interesting trinkets.

Street Food
Don't forget to grab a bite from one of the numerous food vendors. I heartily recommend the coconut ice cream and Thai iced tea—both

refreshing and delicious after a long day of shopping!

Damnoen Saduak Floating Market

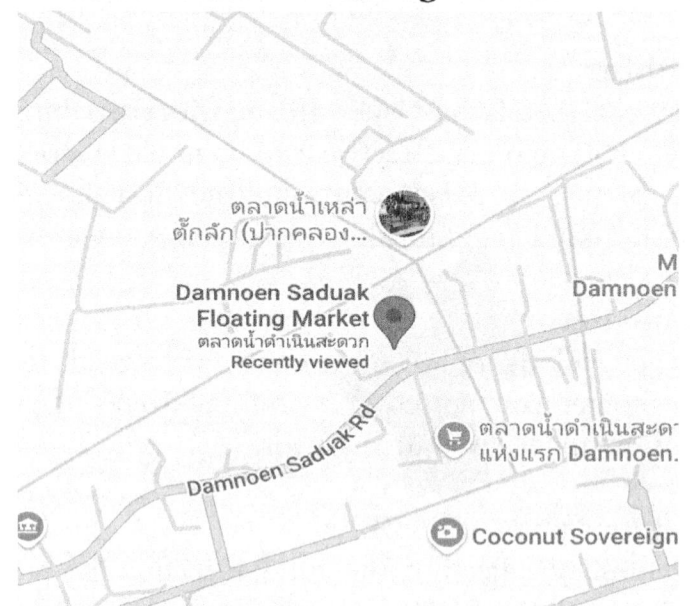

If you've ever seen a postcard from Thailand, chances are it depicts a bright scene from a floating market. The Damnoen Saduak Floating Market is one of the most well-known, and it offers a unique glimpse into traditional Thai business. Located approximately an hour outside of Bangkok, this market is still highly active, especially in the mornings.

What To Buy

Fresh Produce
Boats are piled high with tropical fruits such as mangos, pineapples, and coconuts. If you enjoy fresh fruit, this is your paradise.

Traditional Thai Appetizers
You can get a variety of appetizers, including grilled satay skewers and sweet coconut pancakes (khanom krok).

Handmade Crafts
Throughout the market, sellers sell handmade baskets, hats, and souvenirs. These things are an excellent way to incorporate a piece of Thai workmanship into your house.

Boat Rides
While visiting Damnoen Saduak, enjoy a short boat ride around the canals to get a true sense of local

life. It's a great way to enjoy the surroundings while also taking some stunning photographs.

Amphawa Floating Market

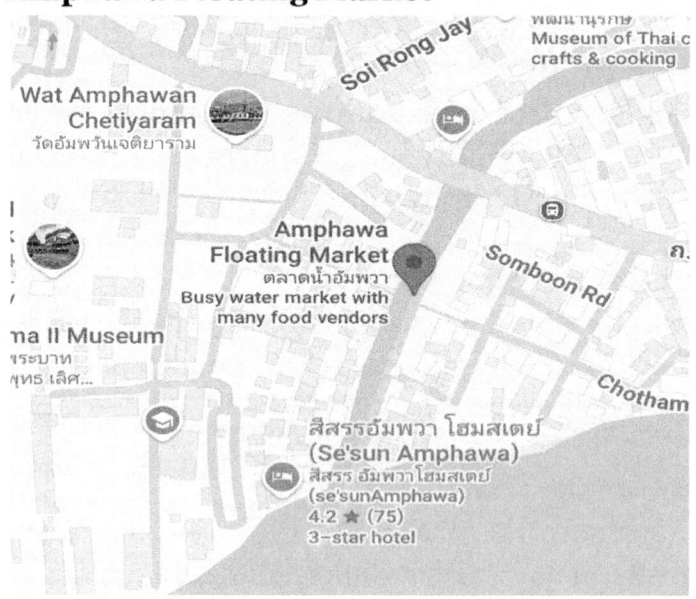

If you're searching for a less touristy floating market, head to Amphawa. Amphawa, located approximately 1.5 hours from Bangkok, has a more local vibe, particularly in the evening when the market comes alive. Unlike Damnoen Saduak, this one remains open later in the evening, making it ideal for a more relaxing evening shopping experience.

What To Buy

Fish
Amphawa is famous for its tasty and fresh fish. Grilled prawns, fish cakes, and fried squid are offered directly from boats along the canals.

Thai Desserts
Sample some traditional Thai desserts like mango sticky rice or Thai coconut custard (khanom thuai). They are an unforgettable pleasure.

Handicrafts & Souvenirs
I discovered stunning handcrafted woodwork things, jewelry, and local artwork. They make ideal mementos and gifts for loved ones.

Pak Klong Talad (Floral Market)

For something completely different, go to Pak Klong Talad, Bangkok's largest flower market. This market is open 24 hours a day and is a riot of color, especially in the early mornings when florists arrive to pick up new blossoms. It's a photographer's dream, with rows upon rows of colorful flowers and plants.

What To Buy

Fresh Flowers
From roses to orchids, there is an astounding selection of flowers available here. I frequently purchase orchids, Thailand's national flower, because they are lovely and survive much longer than other flowers.

Flower Garlands
Are commonly used in religious occasions, but they also make attractive souvenirs. They're made of jasmine, marigolds, and other fragrant flowers and come in bright bundles.

Planting Supplies
If you enjoy gardening, you'll find a wide selection of plants, pots, and gardening tools at affordable prices.

Pratunam Market

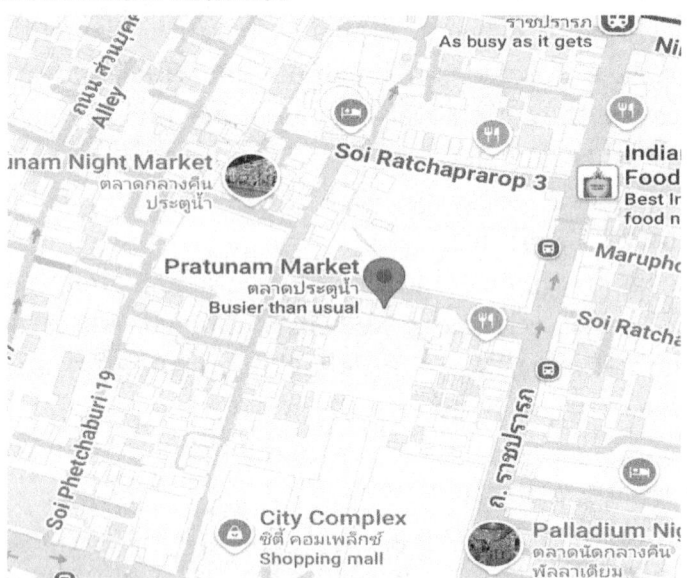

Pratunam Market is a shoppers' paradise for those shopping for low-cost clothes. It's close to the Platinum Fashion Mall and is an excellent spot to get wholesale apparel at low costs. The market might get crowded, but the deals make it worthwhile.

What to Buy?

Clothing
From casual clothing to party outfits, you'll find a wide range of stylish products at extremely affordable costs. Bargaining is widespread, so don't be afraid to ask for a better price.

Accessories
Pratunam also has excellent vendors selling handbags, hats, and scarves.

Modern Malls

Bangkok is an ideal utopia for people like me who value both luxury and convenience. When I want to indulge in high-end products, see gorgeous architecture, or simply escape the city's heat, I visit one of Bangkok's sophisticated shopping malls. Two of my personal favorites, Siam Paragon and CentralWorld, are excellent illustrations of why Bangkok has become a global shopping destination.

Siam Paragon

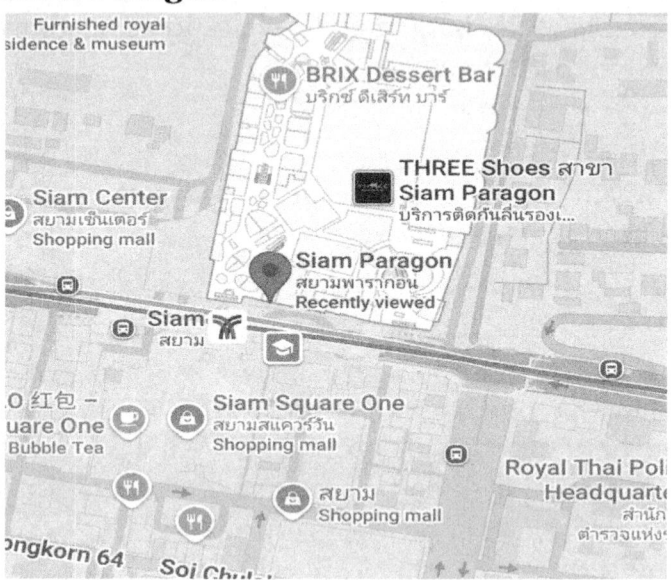

Walking into Siam Paragon feels like entering a world of luxury and style. One of Bangkok's most prominent malls is located right in the heart of the city, near to the Siam BTS station. As soon as I walk in, I'm surrounded by luxury—top worldwide labels like Louis Vuitton, Gucci, and Chanel line the clean corridors, which shine under crystal-clear lighting. Whether I'm window shopping or treating myself to something special, Siam Paragon provides an upscale experience that is difficult to duplicate.

But Siam Paragon offers more than just shopping. If you are a car fanatic, you will enjoy the luxury automobile stores, which feature brands such as Lamborghini and Rolls-Royce. I always make time for the basement floor, which has Siam Ocean World, a gigantic aquarium ideal for kids and curious tourists like myself. Furthermore, the food court here is unparalleled—everything from gourmet meals to quick Thai staples awaits.

CentralWorld
If Siam Paragon represents the pinnacle of luxury, CentralWorld provides a combination of high-end and contemporary shopping options to suit every budget and taste. It's massive—one of Southeast Asia's largest malls—and I can spend hours strolling around without getting bored.

CentralWorld features everything, from flagship stores for major global brands like H&M and Zara to digital products, home décor, and cosmetic businesses. On the higher levels, I enjoy perusing lifestyle businesses and quirky pop-ups where local designers showcase their distinct styles. It's also an excellent spot to eat—CentralWorld's eating options range from chic rooftop restaurants to quaint food stalls selling my favorite Thai dishes.

However, it is the events that actually stick out. Whether it's seasonal festivals, art installations, or live music performances, CentralWorld is always buzzing with activity. During New Year's celebrations, the outdoor plaza transforms into a giant countdown party—something you must see at least once.

Why Bangkok Malls are Unique
What I like best about Bangkok's modern malls is that they're more than just shopping destinations; they're cultural magnets. You can shop, eat, see a movie, or spend hours enjoying the local art installations. These malls are ideal for visitors and expats like myself because they combine modern luxury with Thai warmth. Whether you want to buy a luxury bag or just relax with an iced Thai tea, Siam Paragon and CentralWorld always provide an unforgettable experience.

Unique Souvenirs and Gifts

When it comes to bringing a bit of Bangkok home, the city is brimming with one-of-a-kind souvenirs and thoughtful presents. From traditional Thai silk to intricately crafted handicrafts, there's plenty to suit every taste and budget. Here's what you should look for while searching for keepsakes or gifts for friends and family.

Thai Silk is a Timeless Classic
If there is one thing you should not miss, it is Thai silk, which is undoubtedly Thailand's most famous memento. The fabric's rich texture and brilliant colors make it enticing. I went to the famous Jim Thompson House, the greatest spot to learn about silk's intriguing history. When shopping, seek for silk scarves, pillows, or ties, as these are easy to pack and make excellent gifts. Authenticity is guaranteed by shops such as Jim Thompson outlets and high-quality silk boutiques.

Handicrafts
Bangkok's handicrafts are among the best I've seen, and each one tells a tale. Markets and stores sell

wonderfully carved wooden sculptures, traditional masks, and handcrafted ceramics. For something unique, I purchased a hand-painted Benjarong porcelain cup, a classic Thai pottery with elaborate gold design. Don't miss the Chatuchak Weekend Market or the Bangkok Art and Culture Centre, where artisans demonstrate their skills.

Jewelry and Accessories
Thailand is also known for producing high-quality gemstones and jewelry. If you enjoy dazzle, Bangkok is the location to discover gorgeous sapphires and rubies, which are frequently set in elegant gold or silver designs. I made certain to shop exclusively at respectable places with credentials, as Bangkok's diamond sector is flourishing and competitive. Look for custom-made rings, necklaces, and earrings—they're the ideal blend of elegance and authenticity.

Spices, Snacks and Local Delights
Thai spices and snacks make an excellent present for those seeking something more savory. I couldn't resist purchasing little packets of Thai curry pastes and dried chili peppers to reproduce the flavors of

Bangkok at home. Another favorite of mine is dried mango and tamarind sweets, which make delicious, lightweight keepsakes. These can be found at markets like Or Tor Kor Market or in supermarkets like Big C.

Traditional Clothing and Accessories
If you're seeking for wearable keepsakes, consider traditional Thai attire such as sarongs or fisherman pants. They're lightweight, comfy, and suitable for tropical climates. I purchased a beautifully embroidered sabai (traditional Thai shawl), which serves as both a fashion piece and a cultural statement.

Haggling Tips

When it comes to buying in Bangkok's lively marketplaces, bargaining is more than a talent; it's a cultural experience. From the vast Chatuchak Weekend Market to the thriving Patpong Night Market, negotiating is nearly expected, and believe me, it's easier than you think. As someone who has spent numerous hours perusing these vibrant stalls,

I've learned several proven strategies to help you get the best deals without feeling embarrassed.

Start with a Friendly Attitude
The trick to haggling in Thailand is to be nice and always smile. Thai merchants value good manners and a welcoming demeanor. Before we begin talks, I normally greet them with a friendly "Sawasdee ka" (hello) or a simple grin. Haggling here is not about conflict; it's a playful back-and-forth, so retain a pleasant attitude.

Know the Starting Price
Before jumping in, I prefer to go around the market to get a sense of prices. Let's assume you're looking for a lovely silk scarf or some unique souvenirs—there's a good probability that other vendors are offering comparable products. I start by casually asking sellers about their prices. This establishes a foundation for what I should pay. If you're unsure, starting around 50-60% of the asking price is usually a good bet.

For example, if a merchant asks 400 Baht, I will say, "How about 200 Baht?""We'll take it from there."

Don't show too much Enthusiasm
This tip is invaluable: even if you're madly in love with something, don't let the merchant see it. I've learned the hard way that once you're enamored with a thing, the price becomes non-negotiable. Instead, I maintain a casual tone and appear uncertain, as if I might walk away.

Use the Walk Away Trick
Walking away is one of the most effective bartering techniques. If the discussions don't go my way, I respectfully thank the vendor and begin to move away gently. They almost always call me back with a lower price. This method works like magic, but I only do it when I'm truly ready to let the object go.

Bundle up for better deals!
Here's a technique I've learned: if I want to buy several goods from the same booth, I'll ask for a discount for combining them. For example, "I'll take two T-shirts and that hat; how much for all of

them?"" Vendors enjoy making more sales, therefore they are frequently eager to drop their prices for bulk purchases.

Cash is King
Most market merchants prefer cash payments, and smaller amounts are your greatest friend. I always carry 20s, 50s, and 100 Baht notes to make negotiating easier. If you hand up a 1,000 Baht note after bartering down to 150 Baht, it will seem awkward and may damage your credibility.

Know when to stop
Finally, keep in mind that a minor price difference may not seem like much to you, but it may be substantial to the vendor. If they're adamant on the pricing and it's still reasonable, I'll usually agree without pushing further. It's about striking a balance that makes both parties satisfied.

Fashion & Design

Bangkok's fashion culture reflects the city's lively vitality, seamlessly blending heritage and innovation. Whether you're meandering through crowded markets or stopping by slick shops, there's always something new to discover in the world of fashion.

One of my favorite aspects of Bangkok is how it has evolved into a hotspot for local designers putting their own distinctive touch on fashion. Many Thai designers appreciate their culture's rich tradition while incorporating contemporary trends to create pieces that are both beautiful and inventive. Designs incorporate traditional Thai textiles such as silk with modern cuts and styles, resulting in a dramatic yet comfortable mix.

Local Designers to Know

Sincere and Sins
This brand is well-known for its innovative designs that combine Thai tradition with worldwide fashion trends. Whether it's a basic dress or a striking

statement item, you can expect to discover high-quality, locally created clothing that combines modern and traditional aspects.

Vatanika
Vatanika's collections are well-known in Bangkok's fashion scene and embody stylish refinement with a hint of aggressiveness. The brand is popular among both residents and celebrities for its elegant yet contemporary designs, which are frequently seen at high-end fashion events.

Disaya
Thai designer Disaya P. founded this brand in 2004, combining whimsical themes with sophisticated tailoring. It's ideal for folks who want attire that feels modern while still retaining femininity and class.

Greyhound Original
Greyhound Original, renowned for its minimalist look, is a must-see for fashion enthusiasts who value simplicity with a twist. Its creations frequently merge Western and Eastern inspirations,

resulting in flexible pieces suitable for both casual and formal events.

Boutiques and Shopping Areas
If you enjoy boutique shopping, the neighborhoods surrounding Siam Square and Thonglor are ideal, as they are home to a variety of tiny, independent businesses that showcase local designers. Siam Center is one of my favorite places to visit—a cutting-edge mall where fashion meets art. Several local boutiques sell one-of-a-kind goods that cannot be found anywhere else.

Chatuchak Market is another must-see destination, recognized not just for its amazing cuisine and antiques, but also for its local fashion finds. Wandering around its countless aisles, you'll discover everything from fashionable streetwear to finely designed purses and jewellery. It's the ideal place to find something unique while also supporting tiny, local craftspeople.

For those looking for something truly unique, I recommend visiting The Commons in Thonglor, a fashionable community mall filled with concept boutiques that combine fashion and lifestyle. You'll find a mix of high-end streetwear and indie labels that are dominating Bangkok's fashion scene.

Fashion that Promotes Sustainability
Sustainability is also gaining hold in Bangkok's fashion industry, and I'm pleased to see more designers and retailers concentrating on environmentally friendly techniques. Many local designers now highlight the use of environmentally friendly materials and ethical production practices, allowing you to shop with conscience.

The Sustainability Shop at Siam Discovery, for example, sells attractive clothing created from recycled textiles and organic materials, as well as eco-friendly accessories and luggage.

Chapter 7: Day Trips and Nearby Destinations

Ayutthaya

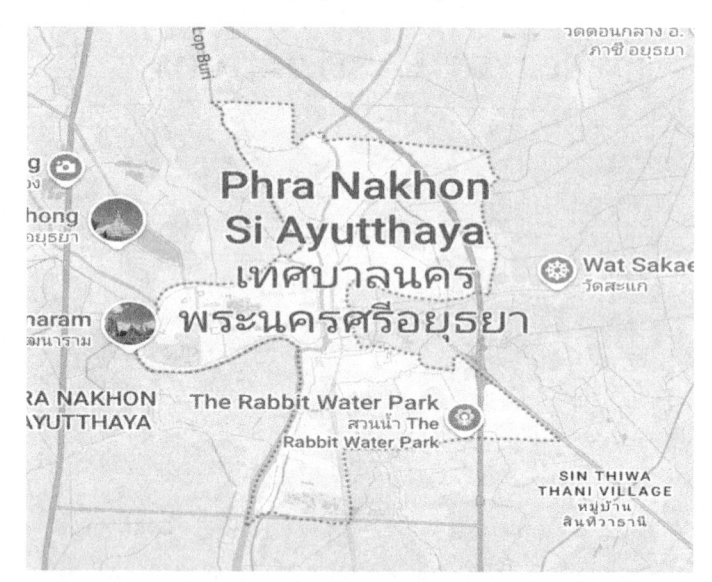

When I first chose to visit Ayutthaya, I was lured by its rich history and the opportunity to wander around the remains of Thailand's once-great city. This UNESCO World Heritage site, located around 80 kilometers north of Bangkok, is a must-see for anybody interested in Thai history, architecture, and culture.

Getting to Ayutthaya

The best way to get to Ayutthaya is via rail, bus, or private automobile, depending on your preferences and travel style. I chose the train since it allowed me to appreciate the scenery while remaining within my budget. The journey from Bangkok's Hua Lamphong Railway Station to Ayutthaya takes around 1.5 to 2 hours, with trains running frequently throughout the day. You can either take a minivan or catch a bus from the Northern Bus Terminal (Mo Chit), which takes around 1.5 hours.

If you want a more deluxe experience, book a private car or a river cruise from Bangkok. Taking a river cruise is not only soothing, but it also provides a unique perspective of the historic temples along the Chao Phraya River.

Exploring The Ruins
When I arrived in Ayutthaya, I was impressed by the contrast between the modern town and the historic remains that bear witness to the city's former splendor. Ayutthaya, built in 1350, was the capital of the Kingdom of Siam and a global commerce hub until it was destroyed by the Burmese in 1767. Despite the devastation, many of

the temples and palaces have been expertly restored, providing insight into what was once one of the world's wealthiest towns.

The Ayutthaya Historical Park serves as the core of the historic city. It is home to spectacular ruins, many of which are temples that have maintained their magnificence. I propose beginning with the most iconic sites such as:

Wat Phra Si Sanphet

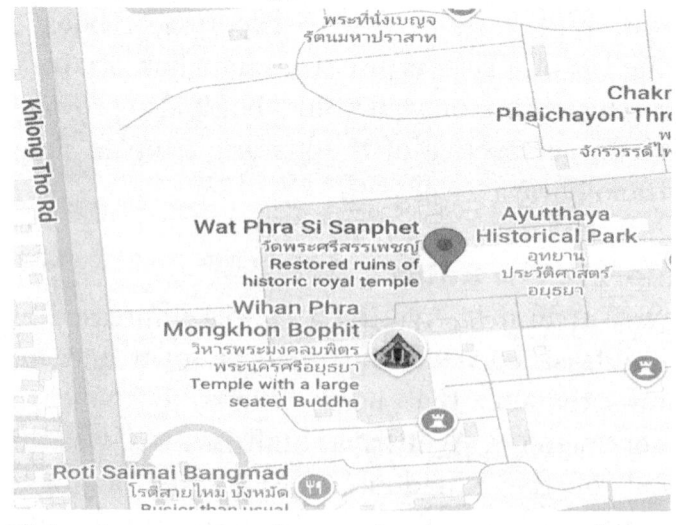

This former royal temple is among the most spectacular. Its three towering chedis (stupas)

dominate the skyline, and the open-air environment allows you to explore at your leisure. It's easy to imagine how this property looked in its peak.

Wat Ratchaburana

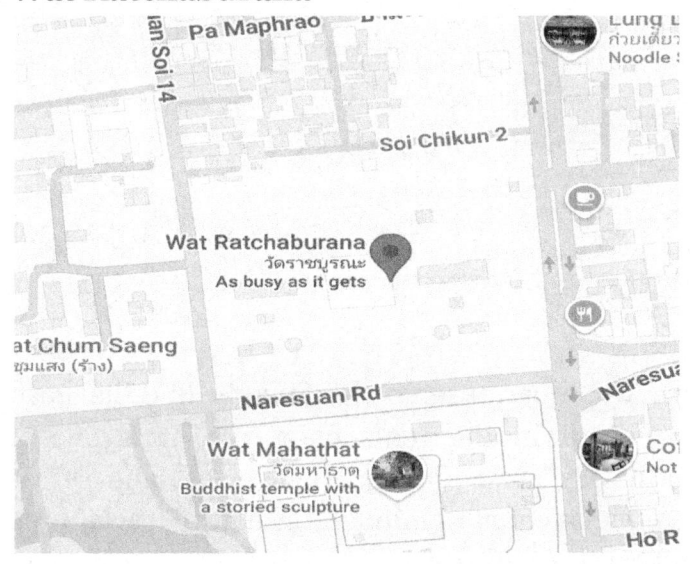

This was one of the most atmospheric temples I saw. The central prang (tower) has been largely rebuilt and features exquisite, detailed reliefs. Despite its history of destruction, I appreciated the sense of tranquility that existed here.

Wat Mahathat

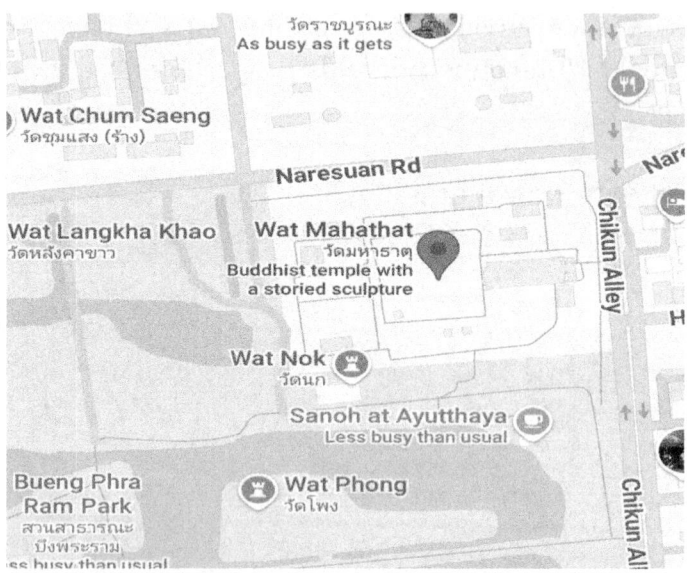

Here you may observe the famous Buddha head intertwined in the roots of a tree. It is one of Ayutthaya's most photographed places and serves as a melancholy reminder of nature reclaiming what was once its own.

To make my visit even more enjoyable, I rented a bicycle from one of the local stores. It's the simplest way to get about the large park and explore at your own time. The heat can be extreme, so carry lots of drinks and take pauses in the shade of the trees.

Visiting By Boat
Another unforgettable way to discover Ayutthaya is by boat. A boat journey down the Chao Phraya River allows you to see the ruins from a whole different angle. There are various boat tours available that take you around the important historical monuments and provide a unique perspective of the temples from the river.

Where To Eat
After a few hours exploring the temples, I was eager to have some great Thai food. There are numerous riverfront restaurants that serve traditional Thai cuisine, but I strongly recommend tasting boat noodles at one of the many small cafés by the water. The thick, fragrant broth and delicate beef served with rice noodles are a local delicacy and one of my favorite meals in Ayutthaya.

For a more premium experience, the Sala Ayutthaya restaurant has a beautiful perspective of the river and is ideal for a relaxing lunch or dinner with a view of the ruins in the background.

When to Visit?

While Ayutthaya is a fantastic location year-round, the ideal months to visit are November and February, when the temperature is cooler and more conducive to exploration. If you visit during the hot season (March to May), expect high temperatures and stay hydrated.

Tips for Visiting

• **Wear comfortable shoes:** The ruins are spread out, and you'll be walking a lot, so decent shoes are essential.

• **Dress modestly:** When visiting temples, remember to cover your shoulders and knees.

• **Pack sunscreen and a hat:** The sun may be harsh, particularly during the dry season.

• **Check for local events:** If your visit coincides with one of Ayutthaya's cultural festivals, it's worth going. The Ayutthaya World Heritage Fair, held in December, is a highlight, with performances, food vendors, and cultural events.

Kanchanaburi

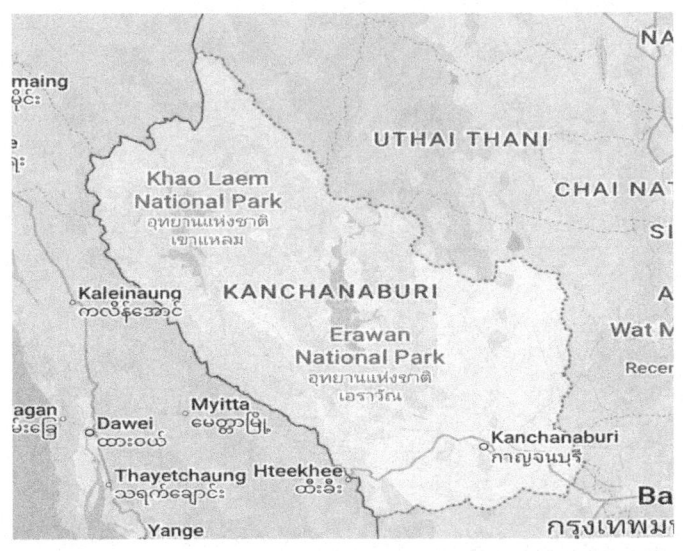

Kanchanaburi is a must-see for history buffs or anyone who enjoys uncovering interesting stories when traveling. Kanchanaburi, located just a few hours west of Bangkok, provides an in-depth insight of Thailand's role in World War II, as well as the breathtaking natural splendor of Erawan National Park.

Bridge over the River Kwai

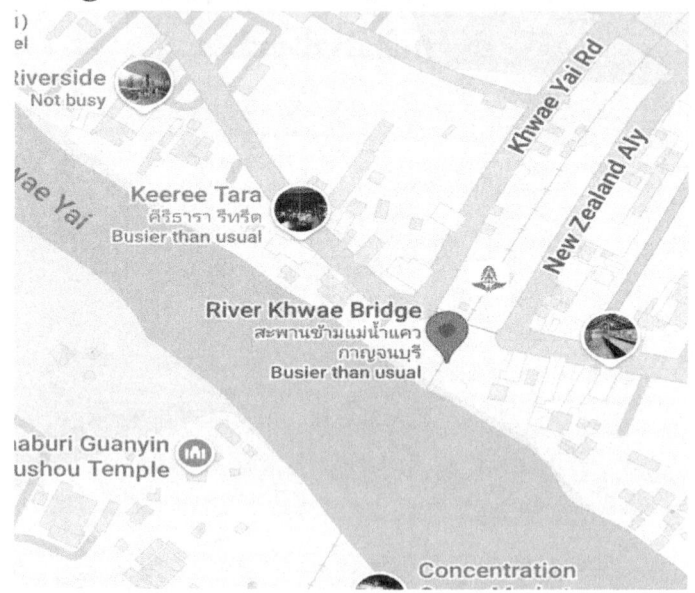

The Bridge Over the River Kwai is one of Kanchanaburi's most prominent historical sites. If you've seen the renowned war movie, you're familiar with the plot, but stepping on the bridge brings history to life. This bridge, originally erected by prisoners of war (POWs) under Japanese supervision during WWII, is part of the Death

Railway, which connected Thailand and Myanmar and played an important role in the Japanese war effort.

As I stood there, I couldn't help but feel the burden of the past. The bridge has been rebuilt since the original was bombed, but it still carries significance, especially when you read about the hardships the POWs faced while building it. I recommend visiting the neighboring War Cemetery, where many POWs who died while building the railway are interred. It's a sobering event, but it helps you grasp the magnitude of the sacrifice and the human cost of war.

The Thai-Burma Railway Centre

A visit to the Thailand-Burma Railway Centre is a fascinating way to learn more about the historical setting. This museum delves deeply into the construction of the Death Railway, featuring relics, photographs, and firsthand tales from POWs. It's quite poignant and well-curated, and I found that it provided me with a much deeper appreciation of the area's significance beyond the bridge alone.

Erawan National Park

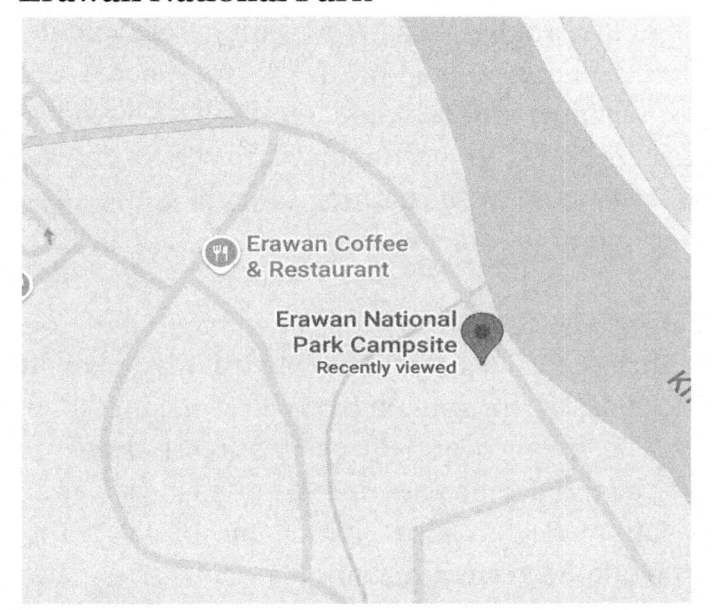

After taking in the history, the next step is to visit Erawan National Park, which is only a short drive from the bridge. It's an ideal respite from the solemnity of ancient places, with lush nature and the magnificent Erawan Falls. The park's seven-tier cascade is breathtaking, with each level offering its own spectacular vista and the opportunity to swim in crystal-clear pools. I took my time hiking up the various levels, admiring the lovely forest and cool water below.

Along the route, I saw a variety of wildlife, including monkeys, and the quiet atmosphere was a nice change from the morning's historical reflections. It's unquestionably a place to unwind and reconnect with nature, providing the ideal counterpoint to Kanchanaburi's melancholy history.

Getting There

Kanchanaburi is easily accessible from Bangkok by train, bus, or private automobile, making it an excellent day or overnight destination. I elected to travel by train, which not only afforded me a view of the landscape but also allowed me to see a tiny portion of the ancient railway.

Pattaya

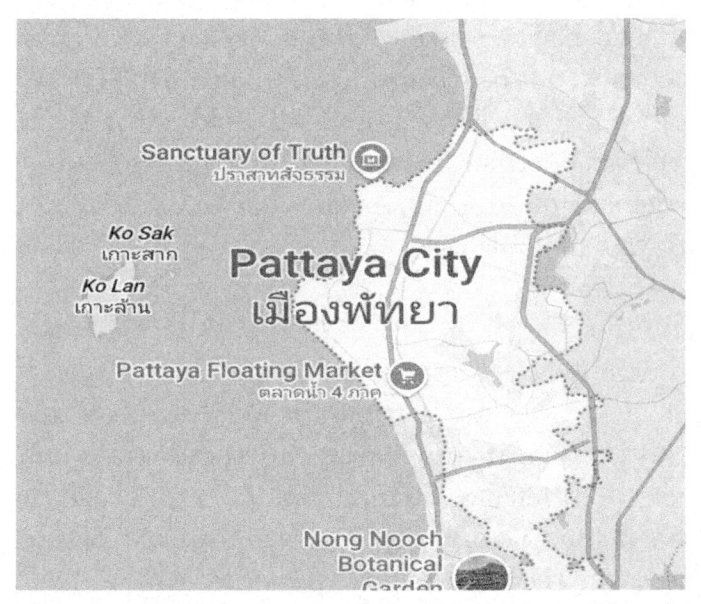

If you want to get away from the rush and bustle of Bangkok, Pattaya is the ideal destination. Pattaya, located just a two-hour drive from Bangkok, provides a refreshing blend of stunning beaches, exhilarating water sports, and a bustling atmosphere that keeps both leisure seekers and adventure enthusiasts coming back for more.

When I first visited Pattaya, I was struck by the contrast between Bangkok's bustling city life and the laid-back seaside ambiance of Pattaya's beaches. The beachfront runs approximately 15 kilometers, providing possibilities for all types of travelers. Whether I wanted to relax in the sun or participate in adrenaline-pumping water activities, Pattaya had it all.

Beaches
Jomtien Beach was one of my favorite places to visit, as it was more tranquil and less busy than Pattaya Beach. If you, like me, appreciate peace and quiet, Jomtien's moderate waves and charming atmosphere make it a great place to relax. Pattaya Beach, on the other hand, provides a more lively atmosphere, allowing people to watch, visit seaside cafés, and wander along the crowded promenade.

For something a little different, I visited Naklua Beach in Pattaya's northern region. It's quieter, with beautiful seas ideal for a swim or a leisurely stroll down the beach. If you're searching for a more relaxed atmosphere, Naklua will not disappoint.

Water Sports
Pattaya is a hotspot for water sports aficionados like me. Whether you're a beginner or a seasoned pro, the possibilities are limitless. I attempted parasailing for the first time here, and it was an amazing experience as I soared above the turquoise waters, taking in panoramic views of the coastline. The thrill of parasailing was followed by jet skiing, another must-do activity for adrenaline enthusiasts. The crystal-clear waters of Pattaya are ideal for these activities, and local operators make safety a top priority.

I also noticed that wind and kite surfing are becoming more popular in Pattaya, with training and equipment available for all skill levels. The Pattaya Floating Market is a great site to arrange trips, rent equipment, or just watch excellent surfers ride the waves.

Island Day Trips
If you're seeking for even more excitement, I highly recommend taking a boat to one of the surrounding islands. Koh Larn, a short boat ride from Pattaya, is known for its crystal-clear waters and beautiful

beaches. I spent the day snorkeling among the coral reefs, observing the beautiful aquatic life. The island also offers kayaking and banana boat trips, which are ideal for families or groups seeking for a fun day on the water.

Damnoen Saduak Floating Market

A visit to the Damnoen Saduak Floating Market, located around 100 kilometers southwest of Bangkok, is one of the city's most famous experiences. As soon as I arrived, I was swept up in the market's vivid energy. The sight of boats carrying colorful fruits, vegetables, and local goods flowing along the small canals, all while vendors shout out to entice clients, is simply breathtaking.

The market, which dates from the nineteenth century, was initially established to connect Thailand's principal canals. While it has evolved to be a popular tourist destination, it nevertheless provides a look into traditional Thai trade. On their wooden boats, sellers sell everything from fresh coconuts and exotic fruits to handmade crafts, souvenirs, and great street cuisine.

I took a boat ride through the canals, which was one of my trip's highlights. The slow-moving boat allowed me to take in the sights and noises, including the chatter of local vendors and the odd honk of passing boats. It seemed like going back in time, watching how people used to trade and interact in this thriving canal economy.

I was also unable to resist the delicious street cuisine on offer. Some of the tastiest Thai appetizers I've ever had were freshly cooked right in front of me. The boat vendors serve everything from pad thai and grilled satay to mango sticky rice, which was the ideal sweet ending to my stay.

While it's a popular tourist attraction, going early in the morning is a wonderful way to avoid crowds. If you want to capture the essence of the market before it becomes too crowded, I recommend arriving at sunrise, when the vendors are setting up and the ambiance is still quiet.

Nakhon Pathom

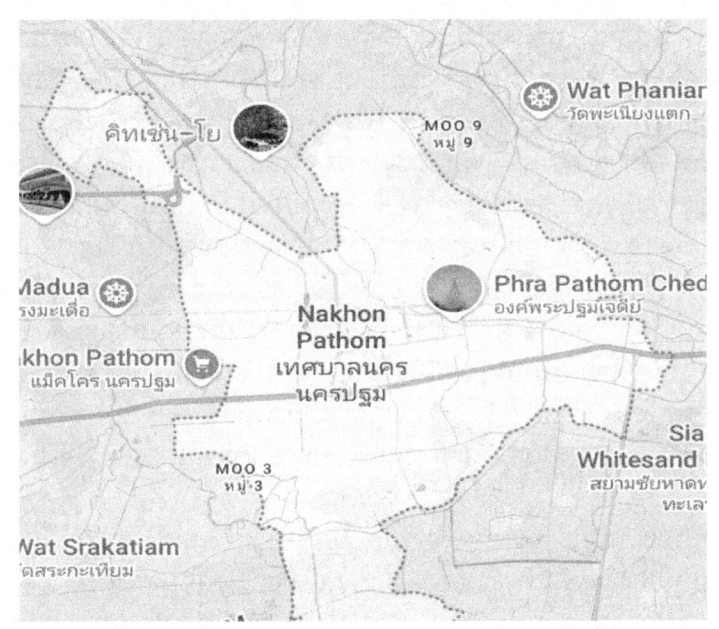

If you want to discover an interesting and little-known jewel near Bangkok, Nakhon Pathom should be on your itinerary. This picturesque region, just an hour's drive from the bustling capital, is home to the world's highest stupa, the Phra Pathom Chedi. Standing at an impressive 127 meters (417 feet), it is an architectural marvel and a testimony to Thailand's rich Buddhist tradition.

The stupa itself is both aesthetically pleasing and spiritually significant. As you approach, the sheer scale of the edifice will take your breath away. The golden dome shines in the sun, while the delicate embellishments on the lower levels showcase centuries of artistry. It is supposed to be Thailand's oldest stupa, going back to the sixth century, and it includes relics thought to be associated with the Buddha himself. Walking around the stupa, you'll notice beautiful walks where residents come to worship, and the atmosphere is serene and reverent, making it an ideal place for introspection.

Other noteworthy sights on the temple grounds emphasize the area's cultural and spiritual significance. You can visit the nearby Sanam Chan Palace, which was originally a royal house but is now a museum. The palace's blend of Thai and European architectural styles stands out and provides a lovely contrast to the stupa's holy mood.

For anyone interested in history and culture, Nakhon Pathom has much more to offer than the Phra Pathom Chedi. It's a tranquil retreat from

Bangkok's fast-paced lifestyle, where you can immerse yourself in Thai customs, visit small local markets, and enjoy regional specialties. The province is rich in agriculture, and you can taste fresh fruits, particularly during the fruit season, when there is a broad selection of tropical goodies available.

Chapter 8: Practical Information for Visitors

Emergency Numbers and Contact Information

When traveling in Bangkok, it's critical to know the local emergency numbers. Knowing who to call in an emergency can make all the difference, so here's a quick rundown of the key phone numbers you'll need on your vacation.

Police – 191
If you are in a situation where you require immediate assistance from the police, phone 191. This number is available 24 hours a day, seven days a week, and the operators speak Thai and some English. Whether it's a theft, an accident, or another type of emergency, this is the number to call for police assistance in Bangkok.

Ambulance – 1554
Health emergencies can occur at any time, so you should know how to contact medical assistance. Call 1554 for an ambulance. Bangkok has a large number of hospitals that provide good care, including international hospitals with English-speaking staff. The response time varies, however contacting this number will link you to medical aid immediately.

Tourist Police – 1155
As a tourist, it's always comforting to know there's a specific line for help. The Tourist Police at 1155 are

available to assist foreigners with any issues, including misplaced passports, frauds, and safety concerns. They are trained to assist in English and will guide you through any problem, so please do not hesitate to contact them if you require assistance.

Currency & Banking

When I initially came to Bangkok, I understood that knowing how to handle money here would make a significant difference in my experience. From finding ATMs to knowing where to exchange currency, it's all part of staying on top of my finances while enjoying everything the city has to offer. Here's what I've learnt about handling money in Bangkok, and I hope it helps you as well!

Currency

Bangkok's currency is the Thai Baht (THB), and while credit cards are widely accepted, cash remains king, particularly at street markets, small shops, and local eateries. I always keep enough cash on hand for my daily transactions.

ATMs
ATMs are widely available in Bangkok, and I found them to be the easiest way to withdraw cash. Most international bank cards function at ATMs, however there is a minor withdrawal fee—usually around 200 THB (around $6) each transaction. To avoid problems, I recommend utilizing ATMs connected to well-known networks such as Citibank or Siam Commercial Bank.

One issue I've discovered is that ATMs in Thailand frequently have withdrawal limitations, which range from 20,000 to 30,000 THB each transaction, so it's worth planning ahead if I need a bigger amount. Also, to minimize surprises, I always verify my bank's foreign transaction costs before withdrawing!

Currency Exchange
If I need to convert money, I go to excellent exchange counters in locations such as Siam Square or MBK Center, where the prices are usually better. Currency exchange shops are also widespread in tourist-friendly districts such as Sukhumvit and Khao San Road, although I advise against

converting at airports because the prices are often lower.

I also keep in mind that it is ideal to exchange Thai Baht before arriving in Bangkok for a better rate, especially if I am traveling from another nation. However, it's always a good idea to have some local cash on hand as soon as I arrive, in case I need to hire a taxi or get a snack.

Tips in Bangkok
Tipping is appreciated in Bangkok, but not required. I've discovered that it is usually a little gesture. For example, I normally leave between 20 and 50 THB for a good lunch at a restaurant, and I occasionally round up the fare when taking a taxi. In more upscale establishments or for exceptional service, I leave more, but the amount is always at my discretion.

Tipping is not expected in cafés or food stalls, but if I have received excellent service or had a positive experience, I will leave some change to express my gratitude. The usual rule is to tip what feels appropriate, taking in mind that many restaurants already add service charges (10-15%) in the bill.

Digital Payments and E-wallets
Bangkok is gradually becoming a cashless culture. I've found that many residents, particularly younger people, utilize apps like GrabPay, LINE Pay, or TrueMoney Wallet to make routine transactions. These e-wallets are frequently accepted in convenience stores, restaurants, and taxis, and I've even used them in tiny shops to speed up payments.

Tourists may use Apple Pay and Google Pay in a variety of venues, but I still prefer to have a mix of cash and digital payment methods on hand just in case.

How to Avoid Scams and Keep Your Money Safe
While Bangkok is typically safe, I've learnt to be cautious with my money. When I'm walking through crowded areas like markets or streets, I keep my wallet in my front pocket or in a safe bag. When I withdraw significant quantities from an ATM, I always do so in daylight or from a well-lit

ATM inside a bank or mall. Furthermore, while using foreign exchange services, I double-check the rate and count my money before departing.

Language & Communication

As a traveler in Bangkok, you'll discover that while many people speak English, particularly in tourist areas, knowing a few basic Thai words will make your trip go much more smoothly and fun. Not only does it demonstrate respect for the local culture, but it also allows for more genuine relationships with the locals. Here's what you should know.

Essential Thai Phrases for Travelers

Hello, Sawasdee (สวัสดี)
Sawasdee is your go-to greeting whether you walk into a store, greet a tuk-tuk driver, or meet a new person. To seem nice, women should add ka (ค่ะ) at the end, while men should say khrap. For example, Sawasdee ka and Sawasdee khrap.

Thank you, Khob Khun (ขอบคุณ)

Expressing thanks goes a long way. To express gratitude for a meal, service, or assistance, say Khob Khun. You can add kap or krap depending on your gender.

Yes, Chai (ใช่)
If you want to confirm or agree, Chai is your word. It's easy to remember!

No, Mai Chai (ไม่ใช่)
Mai Chai is ideal for saying no to anything. You may find yourself utilizing this at food markets to politely decline a meal you are not in the mood for.

How much is this? - What about Nee Tao Rai? (นี่เท่าไหร่)
This phrase is useful when shopping at a market or negotiating prices. Point to the item and ask for a price; you'll get it right away.

Excuse me/Sorry - Kor Toht
If you accidentally run into someone or need to draw their attention, Kor Toht is a polite way to express "excuse me" or "sorry."

Where is [location]? - *[Location] Yoo tee nai? ([สถานที่] อยู่ที่ไหน?)
If you're seeking a specific temple, restaurant, or landmark, you might inquire, "Wat Arun yoo tee nai?" (Where is Wat Arun?) or use the location name as needed.

Pronunciation Tips for Travelers
Thai pronunciation can be challenging since the language is tonal, which means that the meaning of a word varies depending on the pitch or tone used. Thai has five tones: low, middle, high, rising, and falling. Here are a few suggestions to assist you navigate this:

• **Pay close attention:** The greatest approach to pick up on tons is to listen to how native speakers pronounce words. It may take some time, but with practice, you will be able to master it.

• **Tone marks:** In written Thai, tone marks might assist you recognize the correct pronunciation. However, don't be too concerned about flawless tones; the essential purpose is to communicate.

- **Use hand gestures:** When in doubt, don't be hesitant to accompany your words with hand gestures or facial emotions. The locals will appreciate your efforts, even if your pronunciation isn't great.

Helpful Language Tips

- **Keep it simple:** While learning to speak Thai is beneficial, you do not need to be fluent to get by. A few words or phrases can have a significant impact.

- **Be polite:** Thai culture emphasizes respect. Always welcome with a grin and utilize ka or khrap to complete your remarks.

- **Use translation apps:** If you're stuck, don't be afraid to use translation software like Google Translate. Many Bangkok residents will understand if you show them the translation on your phone.

English in Bangkok
There are many English speakers in the key tourist districts, including Sukhumvit, Khao San Road, and Silom. Hotel employees, restaurant workers, and

taxi drivers frequently speak basic English. However, the further you travel from tourist hotspots, the less likely you are to encounter fluent English speakers. Knowing a few Thai terms can make your trip more pleasurable and immersing.

Internet and SIM Cards

When I initially arrived in Bangkok, staying in touch was one of my main goals. Whether I needed to explore the city, communicate with friends and family, or simply update my social media, having consistent internet connectivity was crucial. Fortunately, Thailand provides a variety of handy ways to stay connected, from acquiring SIM cards to accessing free Wi-Fi in almost every area of the city.

Purchase a SIM Card

If you want to stay in Bangkok for more than a few days, getting a local SIM card is the cheapest option to stay connected. The process is straightforward, as SIM cards are accessible at both Suvarnabhumi and Don Mueang Airports as soon as you arrive. I personally chose a prepaid SIM card since it offers flexibility without the necessity for a long-term commitment. The major providers—AIS, DTAC, and TrueMove—all give a variety of plans, including data, talk time, and text packages suited to travelers.

I was able to get a SIM card for as little as THB 100-200 (about $3-6 USD), which provided me with plenty of data and minutes for calls. These SIM cards are incredibly convenient because they can be recharged at local convenience stores or online using mobile banking apps.

To purchase a SIM card, all you need is your passport because The law demands registration. The staff at the kiosks or airport counters will help you set everything up, including activating the SIM card in your phone. Within minutes, I was ready to go!

Free Wi-Fi in Bangkok
In addition to a SIM card, I discovered that free Wi-Fi was readily available throughout Bangkok. Major retail malls such as Siam Paragon, CentralWorld, and MBK all provide free Wi-Fi to

guests. The same is true for numerous restaurants, cafes, and even some street vendors. It's an excellent approach to save data if you solely use maps or social media while on the go.

Most public parks and government buildings offer free Wi-Fi, as do several public transportation systems such as the BTS Skytrain and the Chao Phraya Express Boat. Connecting is frequently as simple as entering an email address or logging in with Facebook.

Tips For Staying Connected

Data Speed
Although 4G/LTE is commonly available, speeds vary depending on your location in the city. In tourist-heavy locations, you'll generally find a strong connection, but in quieter, residential neighborhoods, the signal may be sluggish.

SIM Card Activation
If you purchase a SIM card at the airport, ensure it is activated before leaving the counter. You don't want to be without service once you're in the city.

Use Wi-Fi Calling
If you don't have a strong signal, consider using services like WhatsApp, Skype, or FaceTime to make calls via Wi-Fi. It's an excellent technique to save money on international phone calls.

Public Holidays and Festivals

Bangkok is a dynamic city, and part of that energy stems from the many festivals and public holidays held throughout the year. Whether you're visiting or planning a longer stay, it's critical to understand the significance of these events and how they may affect your travel arrangements. Here are some of the main holidays and festivals to expect this year.

Songkran - Thai New Year (April 13–15)
Songkran is Thailand's most famous celebration, celebrating the Thai New Year. It's a lively and traditional festival that offers one of the best opportunities to explore Bangkok's vibrant street culture. Expect water fights in the streets, parades, and pilgrimages to temples for prayers and blessings. If you're visiting Bangkok during

Songkran, be prepared to be soaked! It is advisable to plan ahead of time by reviewing water fight zones and preparing for potential road closures, particularly along Khao San Road.

Loy Krathong (November)
Loy Krathong is another major Thai celebration. Traditionally, people make miniature boats (krathongs) out of banana leaves, flowers, and candles and release them into rivers or canals to honor water spirits. The Chao Phraya River in Bangkok is lined with spectacular displays that are a sight to behold. Be aware, however, that transportation in and around river regions might become congested as both locals and tourists converge to celebrate. If you intend to participate, now is a good time to take a river cruise or visit temples such as Wat Arun for a more peaceful experience.

King Maha Vajiralongkorn's birthday is July 28
This national holiday commemorates the birthday of the current monarch, King Maha Vajiralongkorn. It is a day of national pride and respect, with rituals

and celebrations held throughout Thailand. Bangkok's streets will be decorated with portraits of the king, and you may spot Thais paying honor by wearing yellow, the color associated with the monarchy. Many companies are closed today, making it a quieter day for tourism. However, it's an excellent time to see the city's temples or cultural attractions at a leisurely pace.

Chinese New Year (January/February)
Although not a Thai festival, Chinese New Year is frequently observed in Bangkok, particularly in the busy Chinatown (Yaowarat). The streets are bustling with colorful parades, lion dances, fireworks, and plenty of food. It's a terrific time to visit if you enjoy cultural festivals, but be prepared for packed streets and restaurants, especially along Yaowarat Road. Some shops and marketplaces may close for the holiday, so check beforehand if you have a specific destination in mind.

National Labour Day (May 1)
Labor Day is a public holiday in Thailand where workers are honored, and many Thais take time off to unwind. While it is not as large or celebratory as

other holidays, certain businesses will be closed, particularly in the retail and service sectors. It's an excellent day for peaceful activities in the city, such as visiting museums or meandering around parks.

Buddhist Holidays (various dates)

Buddhism is essential to Thai culture, and several Buddhist holidays are commemorated throughout the year. The most important are Makha Bucha, which celebrates the Buddha's teachings, and Visakha Bucha, which commemorates the Buddha's birth, enlightenment, and death. During these days, temple visits and religious activities may increase. The city is generally peaceful, with many residents participating in prayers and offerings. These are excellent possibilities for travelers seeking to see Thailand's spiritual side.

Planning Around Festivals

If you intend to visit Bangkok over any of these holidays, you must plan ahead of time. Some attractions may close or operate only during certain hours, and public transportation may get packed. Nonetheless, these festivals provide a true experience of Thai culture, and attending them is well worth the effort. Here are a few suggestions to help you navigate:

Accommodation
Book your hotel well in advance for important holidays such as Songkran or Chinese New Year. Prices may escalate during certain periods due to excessive demand.

Transportation
During festivals, public transportation, such as the Skytrain and boats, might get congested or even cease to operate in some regions. To avoid the chaos, consider walking or using a ride-sharing service.

Activities
Some popular attractions, such as temples or marketplaces, may be packed or closed on specific holidays. Check online or ask locals about opening hours.

Dress Modestly

When visiting temples during a holiday or festival, remember to cover your shoulders and knees as a symbol of respect.

Chapter 9: Suggested Itinerary for Bangkok

3-Day Itinerary for First-Time Visitors

If you just have a few days in Bangkok, this is how I recommend you spend them. Each day includes a variety of cultural landmarks, shopping, and dining experiences—after all, Bangkok is all about combining tradition and modernity.

Day 1: Must-See Temples and the Grand Palace

Morning

Begin your day by seeing the Grand Palace and Wat Phra Kaew (the Emerald Buddha Temple). I definitely recommend arriving early to avoid the crowds. For centuries, this breathtaking structure served as the palace of Thai kings, and its intricate architecture and gilded accents will leave you speechless. The Emerald Buddha, despite its diminutive size, is Thailand's most treasured Buddhist icon.

Late Morning

Visit Wat Arun (the Temple of Dawn). Located on the west bank of the Chao Phraya River, this temple's central spire provides breathtaking vistas. The exquisite porcelain features make it an ideal subject for photographers.

Afternoon

After a morning of culture, take a break and have lunch by the river. There are several eateries that provide traditional Thai cuisine while overlooking the ocean.

Evening
A river trip is a great way to end the day. You'll gain a different view on Bangkok as you pass by temples and the metropolitan skyline. I recommend planning a dinner cruise for a relaxed and scenic finale to your first day.

Day 2: Markets, Street Food, and Shopping

Morning
Begin your day by visiting Chatuchak Market (the Weekend Market), which is a must-see if you are in Bangkok on a Saturday or Sunday. It is one of the world's largest outdoor markets, with more than 15,000 stalls selling everything from clothing to antiques and food. Don't forget to acquire some mango sticky rice or pad thai from one of the street sellers.

Afternoon
Spend the afternoon around Siam Square. This shopping zone is home to upscale malls such as

Siam Paragon and MBK Center. Siam has it all, from luxury brands to eccentric local businesses. If you're searching for something more traditional, head to Chinatown's Sampeng Market for a real, crowded shopping experience.

Evening
Visit Asiatique the Riverfront for meals and shopping. This riverfront mall mixes modernity and traditional Thai charm. You can also see a concert at Calypso Cabaret or browse the night market for homemade products.

Day 3: Culture, Food, and Relaxation

Morning
Visit Jim Thompson House to learn about the American entrepreneur who helped revitalize Thailand's silk industry. The house is a calm haven in the heart of the city, with traditional Thai architecture and a beautiful garden.

Afternoon
Visit Lumpini Park for a relaxing stroll. This natural location is ideal for unwinding after several days of

sightseeing. If you feel daring, you can rent a paddleboat on the lake.

Evening
Finish your stay with a wonderful evening in Chinatown (Yaowarat), where you can sample some of Bangkok's best street food. The busy streets are lined with food sellers selling everything from dim sum to fried noodles and shellfish.

7-Day Itinerary for a Deeper Exploration of Bangkok

If you have more time, this seven-day itinerary will show you the best of Bangkok, with an emphasis on more local experiences, hidden jewels, and one-of-a-kind activities.

Day 1: Iconic Sights and River Views
This day is identical to the three-day plan, but you can spend more time at the Grand Palace and Wat Arun, possibly including a visit to Wat Pho, home to the enormous reclining Buddha, before enjoying the river cruise.

Day 2: Markets & Old Town

On Day 2, after seeing Chatuchak Market, spend the afternoon roaming around Rattanakosin Island (Old Town). Khao San Road is known for its backpacker culture and offbeat stores. There are a few other temples nearby, including Wat Saket (Golden Mount) and Loha Prasat (Metal Castle).

Day 3: Shopping and Modern Bangkok

In addition to the retail centers around Siam Square, spend the afternoon at Terminal 21 mall, which is designed after many international capitals. This mall's design makes it a wonderful place to take Instagram shots, and the food court is among the best in Bangkok.

Day 4: Hidden Gems & Traditional Thai Culture

Visit Bang Krachao (also known as the "Green Lung of Bangkok") for a bike ride through beautiful vegetation and quaint Thai villages to experience Bangkok's gentler side. You can also go to Bang Nam Phueng Floating Market for a unique experience.

Day 5: Art & History
Spend your day exploring Bangkok's museums. The Bangkok National Museum provides an in-depth look at Thailand's history, while the Bangkok Art and Culture Center (BACC) exhibits contemporary Thai art. Don't miss the Erawan Shrine, known for its vibrant religious activities.

Day 6: Day Trip to Ayutthaya
Take a day excursion to Ayutthaya, Siam's historic capital, located about an hour and a half from Bangkok. The remains of this UNESCO World Heritage Site are beautiful and provide insight into the city's rich past.

Day 7: Relaxation and Farewell
On your last day, Relax at a spa or attend a traditional Thai cooking lesson to learn how to make your favorite foods. In the evening, have your final meal at a rooftop bar with a view of the city skyline.

Conclusion

As I end this Bangkok guide, I can't help but think about how unique this city is—a combination of vivid turmoil, rich history, and amazing moments around every corner. Whether you've marveled at the Grand Palace's sparkling spires, browsed through lively street markets, sampled the amazing tastes of pad Thai on a roadside stall, or watched the sunset over the Chao Phraya River, I hope this guide has been a reliable friend.

Bangkok is full of energy and contrasts, with centuries-old temples standing proudly next to soaring skyscrapers and the peacefulness of a monk's morning chant blending in with the boisterous clamor of night markets. I've always believed that each tourist to Bangkok has a unique experience, which is part of its allure. It's a city where you can create your own trip, whether you're a first-time visitor looking for renowned landmarks or returning for deeper cultural immersion.

I've tried to provide you not only practical advice, but also a sense of what makes Bangkok genuinely unique: its people, food, customs, and ever-changing pulse. Remember that the heart of this city is found not only in its landmarks, but also in its lanes, floating markets, little cafés, and the daily lives of those who live there.

As you pack your luggage or finish the last page of this guide, remember that Bangkok will always welcome you back. No matter how many times you go, there is always something new to discover—another street you haven't strolled down, a food you haven't tried, or a tale waiting to be told.

Printed in Great Britain
by Amazon